This collection
belongs to

sophie Heron

Published by Ladybird Books Ltd 2012
A Penguin Company
Penguin Books Ltd, 80 Strand, London, WC2R 0RL, UK
Penguin Group (USA) Inc., 375 Hudson Street, New York 10014, USA
Penguin Books Australia Ltd, Camberwell Road, Camberwell, Victoria 3124,
Australia (A division of Pearson Australia Group Pty Ltd)
Canada, India, New Zealand, South Africa

Sunbird is a trademark of Ladybird Books Ltd

Written by Richard Dinnick
Photography by Neil Hall
All figures are accurate at time of going to print. Some figures may be withdrawn from the
market at any time. Some may not be available to all markets /retailers / territories.

www.ladybird.com

ISBN: 978-1-40939-178-4
001 - 10 9 8 7 6 5 4 3 2 1
Printed in China

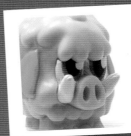

The Official
COLLECTABLE
FIGURES GUIDE

SUNBIRD
PENGUIN

Contents

Series One

Series Two

Series Three

Series Four

Contents

Welcome, Collectors!

Is I.G.G.Y. available in Special Gold? Who will you find in a
Moshi Surprise Egg? Which are the **rarest of the rare,**
and which glow-in-the-dark?
The answers to all of these questions are here, in
The Official Collectable Figures Guide.

Use this book to **keep track of your collection** and learn about each
one along the way. If you're having difficulty finding certain figures, you'll
be able to **tell at a glance** which ones are difficult to find, and which
are quite common, or just a purchase or swap away. Some variations even
go for **megabucks** on online auction sites, so **keep an eye out** for the
super rare and hang on tight to those!

We've listed all the **characters by series** and on each page you'll find
information about them as well as things to look for on the figures and,
most importantly, information on which figures come in which variations.
You can also get a **sneak preview** of figures that haven't even hit the
shelves yet, so you can be ready to search for them!

So what are you waiting for?
Dive in and check your collection!

Pixel-Munching Snafflers have a real problem. They **find cursors really irritating** – like bugs droning around their heads. But they can't use a fly swat or a rolled-up newspaper as they don't have any arms! So **they munch 'em** instead. **Gulp!**

Because of their spiky, fluffy hair, you will sometimes see a Pixel-Munching Snaffler **trapped in a hedge or bush**, tangled in the twigs. But this is quite rare because they can use **strange portals** in cyberspace called Aargates to whoosh around Monstro City. Experts believe this uses a lot of energy, which may explain why they are so **fond of power surges**.

Species: **Pixel-Munching Snaffler**
Set: **Fluffies**
Number: **100**
Rarity: **Ultra Rare**
Variations: **20**

Ultra Rare

Things to look for:
Spiky hair, goggle-eyes, cheesy grin.

What are they like?
Random, overexcited, bouncy and hungry!

Classic/Ultimate Collection
Blind Bag Collectors Pack

Where to find 'em:

Ultra Rare

Glitter Purple
Blind Bag/Collectors Pack

Glitter Orange
Blind Bag/Collectors Pack

Special Gold
Blind Bag/Collectors Pack/
Collector Tin 1

Glow-in-the-Dark
Scream Green
Halloween

Glow-in-the-Dark
Voodoo Blue
Halloween

Glow-in-the-Dark
Ghost White
Halloween

Ultra Rare

Special
Pumpkin Heads
Halloween

Ultra Rare

Green Two-Tone Swirl
Super Seeds

Ultra Rare

Red/Yellow
Two-Tone Swirl
Super Seeds

Frostbite Blue
Winter Wonderland

Ultra Rare

Bauble Red
Winter Wonderland

Ultra Rare

Limited Edition
Goshi Moshi Blue
Goshi Moshi Tin

Ultra Rare

Goo Green
Moshi Goo

Ultra Rare

Special Edition Advent
Advent Calendar

Christmas Tree Green
Winter Wonderland

Brilliant Blue
Moshi Surprise Egg 2012

Shocking Pink
Moshi Surprise Egg 2012

Sonic Orange
Moshi Surprise Egg 2012

Electric Yellow
Moshi Surprise Egg 2012

Angel

Species: SkyPony
Set: Ponies
Number: 024
Rarity: Common
Variations: 20

☑

SkyPonies are **the stuff of legend** in Monstro City. Everyone **thought they were extinct** until an entire herd of the creatures appeared on a pink cloud called Cloud Nine, high above Mount Sillimanjaro. These **heavenly horses** often hang out there but they also enjoy flapping through the **Airy Fairy Plains.**

Wherever you find them, SkyPonies will often be **playing the harp** or slurping their favourite food: maple syrup! Whatever you do, don't put a saddle on them because **they hate saddlebags**. They're not fond of sharp things either – especially drawing pins . . .

What are they like?
Fluffy, elegant, airborne and mysterious!

Things to look for:
Wings, horn, star, tail.

Classic/Ultimate Collection
Blind bag/collectors pack

Where to find 'em:

Ultra Rare

Glitter Purple
Blind Bag/Collectors Pack

Glitter Orange
Blind Bag/Collectors Pack

Special Gold
Blind Bag/Collectors Pack/
Collector Tin 1

Glow-in-the-Dark Scream Green
Halloween

☑

Glow-in-the-Dark Voodoo Blue
Halloween

Glow-in-the-Dark Ghost White
Halloween

Ultra Rare

Special Pumpkin Heads
Halloween

☑

Ultra Rare

Twistmas Edition
Advent Calendar

Ultra Rare

Red/Yellow Two-Tone Swirl
Super Seeds

Frostbite Blue
Winter Wonderland

Ultra Rare

Bauble Red
Winter Wonderland

Ultra Rare

Limited Edition Goshi Moshi Blue
Goshi Moshi Tin

Ultra Rare

Goo Green
Moshi Goo

Ultra Rare

Green Two-Tone Swirl
Super Seeds

Christmas Tree Green
Winter Wonderland

Electric Yellow
Moshi Surprise Egg 2012

Brilliant Blue
Moshi Surprise Egg 2012

Shocking Pink
Moshi Surprise Egg 2012

Sonic Orange
Moshi Surprise Egg 2012

Stanley

Species: Songful SeaHorse
Set: Fishies
Number: 018
Rarity: Common
Variations: 19

√

What are they like?
Flashy, tactless and deafeningly raucous!

Things to look for:
Whistling mouth, wiggling tail, big eyes, cute ears.

There's a reason the Songful SeaHorses are called songful: they can't stop whistling **seriously annoying show tunes** at top volume. Strangely, although they may look a bit like them, they really dislike Kazoos. When they whistle their tunes, they usually **do a little dance and blow bubbles** in the water, which is very cute!

Songful SeaHorses **aren't very good at swimming** and tend to hang around in the shallow end of the ocean – mostly around Reggae Reef. Although Songful SeaHorses love a good tune, they really dislike serious opera. They are also not fond of bubble bath, as all those frothy bubbles tickle their snouts!

Classic/Ultimate Collection
Blind Bag/Collectors Pack

Where to find 'em:

Ultra Rare
Glitter Purple
Blind Bag/Collectors Pack

Glitter Orange
Blind Bag/Collectors Pack

Special Gold
Blind Bag/Collectors Pack/
Collector Tin 1

Christmas Tree Green
Winter Wonderland

Glow-in-the-Dark Scream Green
Halloween

Glow-in-the-Dark Voodoo Blue
(Halloween)

Glow-in-the-Dark Ghost White
Halloween

Ultra Rare
Special Pumpkin Heads
Halloween

Ultra Rare
Green Two-Tone Swirl
Super Seeds

Ultra Rare
Red/Yellow Two-Tone Swirl
Super Seeds

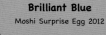
Frostbite Blue
(Winter Wonderland)

Ultra Rare
Bauble Red
Winter Wonderland

Ultra Rare
Limited Edition Goshi Moshi Blue
Goshi Moshi Tin

Ultra Rare
Goo Green
Moshi Goo

Brilliant Blue
Moshi Surprise Egg 2012

Shocking Pink
Moshi Surprise Egg 2012

Sonic Orange
Moshi Surprise Egg 2012

Electric Yellow
Moshi Surprise Egg 2012

Purdy

Species: **Tubby Huggishi**
Set: **Kitties**
Number: **020**
Rarity: **Common**
Variations: **17**

These shaggy kitties are one of the most huggilicious kinds of Moshling in Monstro City. They're **adorable and they know it!** They spend almost all day washing their coats, and making sure they look just right! That's why they **hate water pistols.**

When they're not **primping and preening** they're found chowing down on cakes and pastries, washed down with gallons of condensed milk. Perhaps that's why **these critters are so cuddly!** The rest of the time they enjoy **lying around on cushions** in OuchiPoo Park by the Candy Cane Caverns.

What are they like?
Greedy, dozy, greedy, gossipy, loveable and did we mention greedy?

Things to look for:
Pretty bow, cuddly tummy, fluffy tail, whisker freckles.

Classic/Ultimate Collection
Blind Bag/Collectors Pack

Where to find 'em:

☐

Ultra Rare

Glitter Purple
Blind Bag/Collectors Pack

☐

Glitter Orange
Blind Bag/Collectors Pack

☐

Ultra Rare

Special Pumpkin Heads
Halloween

☐

Glow-in-the-Dark Scream Green
Halloween

☑

Glow-in-the-Dark Voodoo Blue
Halloween

☑

Glow-in-the-Dark Ghost White
~~Halloween~~

☐

Ultra Rare

Red/Yellow Two-Tone Swirl
Super Seeds

☐ **Ultra Rare**

Green Two-Tone Swirl
Super Seeds

☐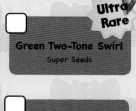

Special Gold
Blind Bag/Collectors Pack/ Collector Tin 1

☑

Frostbite Blue
~~Winter Wonderland~~

☐

Ultra Rare

Bauble Red
Winter Wonderland

☐

Christmas Tree Green
Winter Wonderland

☐

Brilliant Blue
Moshi Surprise Egg 2012

☐

Shocking Pink
Moshi Surprise Egg 2012

☐

Sonic Orange
Moshi Surprise Egg 2012

☐

Electric Yellow
Moshi Surprise Egg 2012

Sooki-Yaki

Species: **Caped Assassin**
Set: **Ninjas**
Number: **047**
Rarity: **Uncommon**
Variations: **17**

☑

Things to look for:
Ninja hood, alert eyes,
sleek tail, powerful paws.

What are they like?
Stealthy, quick,
clever and fleeting.

Classic/Ultimate Collection
Blind Bag Collectors Pack

The Caped Assassins are **agile little Moshlings** who can vanish and reappear in an instant. The trouble is they have **no control** over when this happens. When they do manage to hang around, they love nothing more than to check out the latest *Gadget Magazine* while **knitting up a new Ninja hood.**

If you do want to see one, head for **East Grumble**. If you're lucky you might see one suddenly appear halfway up a drainpipe! Why a drainpipe? Because they **hate slippery roof tiles** and will do anything to avoid them.

Where to find 'em:

Ultra Rare

Glitter Purple
Blind Bag/Collectors Pack

Glitter Orange
Blind Bag/Collectors Pack

Special Gold
Blind Bag/Collectors Pack/
Collector Tin 1

✓

**Glow-in-the-Dark
Scream Green**
Halloween

**Glow-in-the-Dark
Voodoo Blue**
Halloween

**Glow-in-the-Dark
Ghost White**
Halloween

Ultra Rare

Special Pumpkin Heads
Halloween

Ultra Rare

Green Two-Tone Swirl
Super Seeds

Ultra Rare

**Red/Yellow
Two-Tone Swirl**
Super Seeds

Frostbite Blue
Winter Wonderland

✓

Ultra Rare

Bauble Red
Winter Wonderland

Brilliant Blue
Moshi Surprise Egg 2012

Shocking Pink
Moshi Surprise Egg 2012

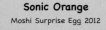

Sonic Orange
Moshi Surprise Egg 2012

Electric Yellow
Moshi Surprise Egg 2012

Christmas Tree Green
Winter Wonderland

Cali

Species: **Valley Mermaid**
Set: **Fishies**
Number: **072**
Rarity: **Rare**
Variations: **17**

So these Valley Mermaids are, **like, way cool.** They totally **hang out in the Sea Mall** beneath the Potion Ocean, OK? And they're so into the **latest koi bands** – Valley Mermids think they are majorly radical.

Think you'll see these babes **rummaging in jumble sales?** As if! Check the local Starfishbucks where they'll be **sipping cappuccinos** and munching seaweed sandwiches or **hooking up their gnarly friends** using their romance detector hearts.

What are they like?
Totally ditsy, way feisty and so cool!

Things to look for:
Heart romance detector, cute headband, awesome tail and luscious locks.

Classic/Ultimate Collection
Blind Bag Collectors Pack

Where to find 'em:

☐
Ultra Rare
Glitter Purple
Blind Bag/Collectors Pack

✓
Glitter Orange
Blind Bag/Collectors Pack

☐
Glow-in-the-Dark Scream Green
Halloween

☐
Ultra Rare
Bauble Red
Winter Wonderland

☐
Glow-in-the-Dark Voodoo Blue
Halloween

☐
Glow-in-the-Dark Ghost White
Halloween

☐
Ultra Rare
Special Pumpkin Heads
Halloween

☐
Christmas Tree Green
Winter Wonderland

☐
Ultra Rare
Red/Yellow Two-Tone Swirl
Super Seeds

✓
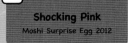
Frostbite Blue
Winter Wonderland

☐
Brilliant Blue
Moshi Surprise Egg 2012

☐
Shocking Pink
Moshi Surprise Egg 2012

☐
Ultra Rare
Green Two-Tone Swirl
Super Seeds

☐
Sonic Orange
Moshi Surprise Egg 2012

☐
Electric Yellow
Moshi Surprise Egg 2012

☐
Special Gold
Blind Bag/Collectors Pack/
Collectors Tin 1

Oddie

Species: **Sweet Ringy Thingy**
Set: **Foodie**
Number: **088**
Rarity: **Ultra Rare**
Variations: **20**

What are they like?
Sweet, animated and cautious.

Ultra Rare

Classic/Ultimate
Collection
Blind Bag Collectors Pack

Things to look for:
Hundreds and thousands, dripping icing, alert eyes and that round hole.

Sweet Ringy Things **love words beginning with 'o'.** Other occupants of Monstro City often want to eat these **tasty offerings** so it's handy that they have an offensive capability - they can defend themselves by firing off **showers of sugary hundreds and thousands.** This prevents them from being dunked in coffee, which is the drink they despise most in the world.

No one knows how these Moshlings came to be, but some think they were **formed in the boiling oil swamps** close to Greasy Geezer. This is why they love the stuff so much. Despite this speculation, we still **don't know who decorates them.** For now it must remain a mystery . . .

Where to find 'em:

Glitter Purple
Blind Bag/Collectors Pack

Ultra Rare

Glitter Orange
Blind Bag/Collectors Pack

✓

Special Gold
Blind Bag/Collectors Pack/
Collector Tin 2

Glow-in-the-Dark Scream Green
Halloween

Glow-in-the-Dark Voodoo Blue
Halloween

Glow-in-the-Dark Ghost White
Halloween

Ultra Rare

Special Pumpkin Heads
Halloween

No Longer Available

Glitter Red *Moshi Magazine* Exclusive
Covermount for Issue 11

Ultra Rare

Red/Yellow Two-Tone Swirl
Super Seeds

Frostbite Blue
Winter Wonderland

Ultra Rare

Bauble Red
Winter Wonderland

✓

Ultra Rare

Twistmas Edition
Advent Calendar

Ultra Rare

Green Two-Tone Swirl
Super Seeds

Brilliant Blue
Moshi Surprise Egg 2012

Shocking Pink
Moshi Surprise Egg 2012

Christmas Tree Green
Winter Wonderland

Rox Collection 2
Rox Tin 2013

Sonic Orange
Moshi Surprise Egg 2012

Electric Yellow
Moshi Surprise Egg 2012

DJ Quack

Species: **Disco Duckie**
Set: **Birdies**
Number: **013**
Rarity: **Common**
Variations: **12**

☑

What are they like?
Rhythmic, big-headed and completely quackers!

Things to look for:
Cool shades, little wings and tiny beak.

Classic
Blind Bag Collectors Pack

Disco Duckies are **dancing divas!** They love nothing more than boogying under a glitter ball, strutting their stuff and busting moves. **Music is their madness** and you can often see them **quacking in time to the beat**. In fact, one thing they can't stand is silence! The other is getting peanut butter stuck in their beaks. That's **gooey not groovy!**

They keep themselves looking good by **slicking their feathers with orange sauce.** If you ever meet one in a dark alley, be sure to duck! They can't see a thing in their shades! Mostly, though, Disco Duckies **jive and moonwalk on the TakiTaki Islands** in the middle of Lake Neon Soup.

Where to find 'em:

☑ **Ultra Rare**

Glitter Purple
~~Blind Bag/~~Collectors Pack

☐

Glitter Orange
Blind Bag/Collectors Pack

☑

Special Gold
Blind Bag/Collectors Pack/
Collector Tin 1

☐

Glow-in-the-Dark
Scream Green
Halloween

☐

Glow-in-the-Dark
Voodoo Blue
Halloween/Spooky Egg

☐

Glow-in-the-Dark
Ghost White
Halloween/Spooky Egg

☐

Sonic Orange
Moshi Surprise Egg 2012

☐

Shocking Pink
Moshi Surprise Egg 2012

☐

Ultra Rare

Special Pumpkin Heads
Halloween

☐

Goo Green
Moshi Goo

☐ **Ultra Rare**

Limited Edition
Goshi Moshi Blue
Goshi Moshi Tin

Squidge

Species: **Furry Heebee**
Set: **Spookies**
Number: **008**
Rarity: **Common**
Variations: **10**

Things to look for:
Leathery wings, radar ears, sweet cheeks and tufty hair.

What are they like?
Diabolical, creepy, deceptive and sharp-toothed!

Classic
Blind Bag/Collectors Pack

If you love **long, black capes** and **creepy organ music**, you'll find a friend in a Furry Heebee. But be careful, these cute-looking Moshlings could give you a **nasty nip** if they're feeling peckish. The best defence is to offer them a **nice, hot mug of tomato soup.**

If you really want to hunt down these greedy bloodsuckers then you'll need to **brave the Crazy Caves** of Fang-Ten Valley. Here you'll see the Furry Heebees **hanging upside down** during the day and flying around at night, squeaking out their **high-pitched cackles!**

Where to find 'em:

Ultra Rare

Glitter Purple
Blind Bag/Collectors Pack

Glitter Orange
Blind Bag/Collectors Pack

Special Gold
Blind Bag/Collectors Pack

Glow-in-the-Dark Scream Green
Halloween

Glow-in-the-Dark Voodoo Blue
Halloween/Spooky Egg

Glow-in-the-Dark Ghost White
Halloween/Spooky Egg

Ultra Rare

Special Pumpkin Heads
Halloween

Shocking Pink
Moshi Surprise Egg 2012

Sonic Orange
Moshi Surprise Egg 2012

27

Priscilla

Species: **Princess Pony**
Set: **Ponies**
Number: **048**
Rarity: **Uncommon**
Variations: **11**

What are they like?
A bit snooty, fickle, magical and proud.

Things to look for:
Sparkling tiara, flowing mane, pearl necklace and manicured hooves!

Classic/Ultimate Collection
Blind Bag/Collectors Pack

Supposedly **descended from royalty,** Princess Ponies actually come from the lowly Old Knackersville, near Gluey Gulch. However, these **haughty horses** are **anything but hum-drum.**

Always straightening their tiaras and waving a regal hoof at people, Princess Ponies **strive to be the centre of attention,** winning rosettes whenever they can. If all else fails, there are manes and tails - these Moshlings can change the colour of theirs simply by **jangling their jingly jewellery!**

Where to find 'em:

Ultra Rare

Glitter Purple
Blind Bag/Collectors Pack

Glitter Orange
Blind Bag/Collectors Pack

Glow-in-the-Dark Scream Green
Halloween

Glow-in-the-Dark Voodoo Blue
Halloween/Spooky Egg

Shocking Pink
Moshi Surprise Egg 2012

Glow-in-the-Dark Ghost White
Halloween/Spooky Egg

Special Pumpkin Heads
Halloween

Ultra Rare

Sonic Orange
Moshi Surprise Egg 2012

blue

Rox Collection 1
Rox Tin 2012

Special Gold
Blind Bag/Collectors Pack

Jeepers

Things to look for:
Inky stripes, ticklish tummy and cute as a button nose.

Species: Snuggly Tiger Cub
Set: Beasties
Number: 073
Rarity: Rare
Variations: 11

✓

Classic/Ultimate Collection
Blind Bag/Collectors Pack

What are they like?
Timid, soppy, endearing and soft.

Snuggly Tiger Cubs are **rarely seen** beyond the rich greenery of the Barmy Swami Jungle, but if you were to venture in, you'd probably be able to find them. Not only do they **love listening to loud glam rock**, but their yellow bodies are useless camouflage in the green jungle. This is why they spend a long time **painting camouflage stripes** on themselves with inka-inka juice, squeezed from thumpkin seeds.

When they aren't earning their stripes you might see them sharpening their claws or **licking the dregs from swoonafish tins.** They are shy, but they love having their **tummies tickled!** Just don't show them a flea collar or a water pistol. They will run if you shoot water at them. And so will their stripes!

Where to find 'em:

Ultra Rare

Glitter Purple
Blind Bag/Collectors Pack

Glitter Orange
Blind Bag/Collectors Pack

Special Gold
Blind Bag/Collectors Pack

Glow-in-the-Dark Voodoo Blue
Halloween/Spooky Egg

Glow-in-the-Dark Ghost White
Halloween/Spooky Egg

Ultra Rare

Twistmas Edition
Advent Calendar

Special Pumpkin Heads
Halloween

Ultra Rare

Glow-in-the-Dark Scream Green
Halloween

Sonic Orange
Moshi Surprise Egg 2012

Shocking Pink
Moshi Surprise Egg 2012

Mr Snoodle

Species: **Silly Snuffler**
Set: **Ponies**
Number: **056**
Rarity: **Rare**
Variations: **11**

When it comes to silliness, it's hard to beat the Silly Snufflers. They are **sleepy, slothful and slack**, prefer life in the slow lane and love listening to lullabies. To stop themselves being snaffled up, Silly Snufflers can make monsters and Moshlings alike **simply fall asleep.** One big yawn and they're gone, because while you sleep, off they creep.

These strange Ponies live around Franzipan Farm, where they love to **feast on pumpernickel breadcrumbs,** shuffle about in slow motion and play a medley of ice cream van melodies with their snouts! But be careful! Remember they can make you fall . . . **ZZZzzzzzz**

Things to look for:
Flappy ears, stubby little snout and polka dots.

What are they like?
Sleepy, snuffly and shuffling.

Series One

Classic/Ultimate Collection
Blind Bag/Collectors Pack

Where to find 'em:

☐  **Ultra Rare**
Glitter Purple
Blind Bag/Collectors Pack

☐
Glitter Orange
Blind Bag/Collectors Pack

☐
Glow-in-the-Dark Ghost White
Halloween/Spooky Egg

☐
Glow-in-the-Dark Scream Green
Halloween/Spooky Egg

☐
Glow-in-the-Dark Voodoo Blue
Halloween/Spooky Egg

☐  **Ultra Rare**
Special Pumpkin Heads
Halloween

☐
Sonic Orange
Moshi Surprise Egg 2012

☐
Shocking Pink
Moshi Surprise Egg 2012

☒  **Ultra Rare**
Twistmas Edition
Advent Calendar

☐
Special Gold
Blind Bag/Collectors Pack

33

Coolio

Species: **Magical Sparklepop**
Set: **Foodies**
Number: **052**
Rarity: **Rare**
Variations: **11**

It's never too cold for a Magical Sparklepop. That's why they can be found **chilling out around Knickerbocker Nook** in the Frozen Dessert Desert. It should be obvious why these Moshlings like it freezing! They just love Whaccurrant sauce and crushed nuts, but **aren't too fond of the sun** as it makes them go all gloopy.

The amazing thing about Magical Sparklepops is that when they do need to cool down, they can **generate glittery sparks** that zoom around their delicious swirly ice cream bodies, making them sub-zero once more. **Fab!**

Things to look for:
Delicious swirls, wafer trousers and creamy tip.

What are they like?
Meltable, cool and optimistic.

Classic
Blind Bag/Collectors Pack

Where to find 'em:

Ultra Rare

Glitter Purple
Blind Bag/Collectors Pack

Glitter Orange
Blind Bag/Collectors Pack

Ultra Rare

Special Pumpkin Heads
Halloween

**Glow-in-the-Dark
Scream Green**
Halloween/Spooky Egg

**Glow-in-the-Dark
Voodoo Blue**
Halloween/Spooky Egg

**Glow-in-the-Dark
Ghost White**
Halloween/Spooky Egg

Shocking Pink
Moshi Surprise Egg 2012

Sonic Orange
Moshi Surprise Egg 2012

Rox Collection 1
Rox Tin 2012

Special Gold
Blind Bag/Collectors Pack

Cleo

Species: Pretty Pyramid
Set: Worldies
Number: 080
Rarity: Ultra Rare
Variations: 10

In the Lost Valley of iSissi on the banks of the River Smile, the sun beats down and the Pretty Pyramids can be found **soaking up the rays!** They live an idyllic life, bathing in milk, making pointy sandcastles and **looking for treasure** buried in the desert.

Being well-behaved, all Pretty Pyramids **love their mummies** and like nothing better than munching bunches of grapes and solving riddles. They also love shiny things, especially gold, but these friendly Moshlings really get **hot under the collar** if any of that golden sand gets into their suntan lotion!

What are they like?
Sunny, smiley, fun-loving.

Things to look for:
Sloping sides, regal bow, happy smile and pointy head.

Ultra Rare

36

Classic/Ultimate Collection
Blind Bag/Collectors Pack

Where to find 'em:

☐

Ultra Rare

Glitter Purple
Blind Bag/Collectors Pack

☐

Glitter Orange
Blind Bag/Collectors Pack

☐

Ultra Rare

Special Pumpkin Heads
Halloween

☐

Glow-in-the-Dark Scream Green
Halloween/Spooky Egg

☑

Glow-in-the-Dark Voodoo Blue
Halloween/Spooky Egg

☐

Glow-in-the-Dark Ghost White
Halloween/Spooky Egg

☐

Shocking Pink
Moshi Surprise Egg 2012

☐

Sonic Orange
Moshi Surprise Egg 2012

Special Gold
Blind Bag/Collectors Pack

RGt collession ✓

Mini Ben

Species: Teeny TickTock
Set: Worldies
Number: 097
Rarity: Ultra Rare
Variations: 10

Ultra Rare

CLONG! Teeny TickTocks are the noisy Moshlings that spend their days on the foggy river banks close to Westmonster Abbey. CLONG! They **love fish and chips**, drinking tea and waxing their moustaches!

CLONG! They **chime on the hour** – every hour – and wander about **making their bells go CLONG!** Teeny TickTocks often nibble daintily at cucumber sandwiches and ask everyone the time because they **can't see the clock faces on their heads!** CLONG!

What are they like?
Aristocratic, dapper and eccentric.

Things to look for:
Clock face, wavy moustache and bushy eyebrows.

Classic/Ultimate Collection
Blind Bag/Collectors Pack

Series One

Where to find 'em:

☐

Ultra Rare

Glitter Purple
Blind Bag/Collectors Pack

☐

Glitter Orange
Blind Bag/Collectors Pack

☐

Special Gold
Blind Bag/Collectors Pack/
Collectors Tin 2

☐

Glow-in-the-Dark Scream Green
Halloween/Spooky Egg

☐

Glow-in-the-Dark Voodoo Blue
Halloween/Spooky Egg

☐

Glow-in-the-Dark Ghost White
Halloween/Spooky Egg

☐

Ultra Rare

Special Pumpkin Heads
Halloween

☑

Shocking Pink
Moshi Surprise Egg 2012

☐

Sonic Orange
Moshi Surprise Egg 2012

Pooky

Species: **Potty Pipsqueak**
Set: **Dinos**
Number: **050**
Rarity: **Uncommon**
Variations: **12**

✓

What are they like?
Playful, inventive, silly and in a world of their own.

Things to look for:
Eggshell helmet, dino-tail and wildly imaginative brain!

When it comes to imagination, it's hard to beat a **playful Potty Pipsqueak!** Although you might think that the eggs they wear on their heads are their own, don't be fooled, they actually belong to **Killer Canaries.** But the shells help these Moshlings to pretend they are astronauts, racing drivers and fire fighters.

As the Potty Pipsqueaks come from Make-Believe Valley, they **love to play pretend.** They can often be seen playing in cardboard boxes that they are using as **spaceships, airplanes and army tanks.**

Classic/Ultimate Collection
Blind Bag/Collectors Pack

Where to find 'em:

Ultra Rare

Glitter Purple
Blind Bag/Collectors Pack

Glitter Orange
Blind Bag/Collectors Pack

Glow-in-the-Dark Ghost White
Halloween/Spooky Egg/
Exclusive 2012

Glow-in-the-Dark Scream Green
Halloween/Spooky Egg/
Exclusive 2012

Glow-in-the-Dark Voodoo Blue
Halloween/Spooky Egg

Brilliant Blue
Moshi Surprise Egg 2012

Ultra Rare

Green Two-Tone Swirl
Super Seeds

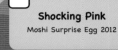

Shocking Pink
Moshi Surprise Egg 2012

Special Gold
Blind Bag/Collectors Pack

Ultra Rare

Special Pumpkin Heads
Halloween 2012

Ultra Rare

Red/Yellow Two-Tone Swirl
Super Seeds

41

Blurp

Species: **Batty Bubblefish**
Set: **Fishies**
Number: **043**
Rarity: **Uncommon**
Variations: **12**

☑

The trouble with Batty Bubblefish is that they are **fantastically forgetful fish.** In fact, they can't remember what it is they've forgotten! This means that they are often alarmed, and when they're frightened, they splurt out **great gallons of multi-coloured gloop.**

When they can remember where they live, these peculiar Moshlings can be found in the foamy waters beneath Fruit Falls. Passers-by often report seeing them pop out of the water, **blow a raspberry** and plop back in again. Here, they swim around holding their breath and looking for old flip-flops.

What are they like?
Forgetful, ornery and easily startled.

Things to look for:
Puffed up body, bubble-blowing lips and spiky defences.

Classic/Ultimate Collection
Blind Bag Collectors Pack

Where to find 'em:

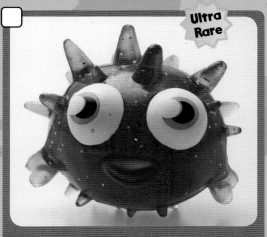

Ultra Rare

Glitter Purple
Blind Bag/Collectors Pack

Glitter Orange
Blind Bag/Collectors Pack

Glow-in-the-Dark Ghost White
Halloween/Spooky Egg/ Exclusive 2012

Ultra Rare

Special Pumpkin Heads
Halloween

Glow-in-the-Dark Scream Green
Halloween/Spooky Egg/ Exclusive 2012

Glow-in-the-Dark Voodoo Blue
Halloween/Spooky Egg

Ultra Rare

Green Two-Tone Swirl
Super Seeds

Shocking Pink
Moshi Surprise Egg 2012

Brilliant Blue
Moshi Surprise Egg 2012

Special Gold
Blind Bag/Collectors Pack

Ultra Rare

Red/Yellow Two-Tone Swirl
Super Seeds

43

Shelby

Species: **Slapstick Tortoise**
Set: **Ninjas**
Number: **039**
Rarity: **Uncommon**
Variations: **12**

Slapstick Tortoises are Ninjas. Well, sort of. They're not very good at it because they always get their moves wrong and **fall over.** They even find it difficult to tie their own bandanas. Unfortunately, Slapstick Tortoises would far rather **watch kung-fu movies** than practise kung-fu moves!

Being tortoises, they **have to hibernate,** and their favourite place for that is under the boardwalk at Groan Bay. During the summertime, they can often be found in groups at the Wailing Wharf. Here they like to **test their skills** (or lack of them!) against other Ninjas.

What are they like?
Clumsy, daft and unfortunate.

Things to look for:
Buck teeth, ninja bandana and polished shell.

Classic/Ultimate Collection
Blind Bag/Collectors Pack

Where to find 'em:

☐

Ultra Rare

Glitter Purple
Blind Bag/Collectors Pack

☐

Glitter Orange
Blind Bag/Collectors Pack

☐

Glow-in-the-Dark Voodoo Blue
Halloween/Spooky Egg

☐

Glow-in-the-Dark Scream Green
Halloween/Spooky Egg/ Exclusive 2012

☐

Glow-in-the-Dark Ghost White
Halloween/Spooky Egg/ Exclusive 2012

☐

Brilliant Blue
Moshi Surprise Egg 2012

☐

Ultra Rare

Green Two-Tone Swirl
Super Seeds

☐ **Special Gold**
Blind Bag/Collectors Pack

☐ **Shocking Pink**
Moshi Surprise Egg 2012

☐

Ultra Rare

Special Pumpkin Heads
Halloween 2012

☐ **Ultra Rare**

Red/Yellow Two-Tone Swirl
Super Seeds

45

Rocky

Species: Baby Blockhead
Set: Worldies
Number: 028
Rarity: Uncommon
Variations: 13

Baby Blockheads live on Beaster Island, where they sit for hours, staring out to sea, listening to rock music and **wondering why they always sink** if they venture into the water! Some Moshlings have tried telling them it's because they're made of stone, but the Baby Blockheads **aren't the sharpest tools in the shed.**

They are very helpful though, and will use their great power to good purpose, **sweating liquid concrete** when they lift heavy objects. They're so strong, you need to be careful when shaking hands, as they can **easily crush your fingers.**

What are they like?
Playful, strong, chirpy and rock-solid!

Things to look for:
Wonky teeth, stony face and googly eyes.

Classic/Ultimate Collection
Blind Bag/Collectors Pack

Where to find 'em:

☐ **Ultra Rare**

Glitter Purple
Blind Bag/Collectors Pack

☐

Glitter Orange
Blind Bag/Collectors Pack

☐

Special Gold
Blind Bag/Collectors Pack/
Collector Tin 2

☐

Glow-in-the-Dark Scream Green
Halloween/Spooky Egg/
Exclusive 2012

☐

Glow-in-the-Dark Voodoo Blue
Halloween/Spooky Egg

☐

Glow-in-the-Dark Ghost White
Halloween/Spooky Egg/
Exclusive 2012

☐ **Ultra Rare**

Special Pumpkin Heads
Halloween

☐

Brilliant Blue
Moshi Surprise Egg 2012

☑ **Ultra Rare**

Twistmas Edition
Advent Calendar

☐

Shocking Pink
Moshi Surprise Egg 2012

☐ **Ultra Rare**

Green Two-Tone Swirl
Super Seeds

☐ **Ultra Rare**

Red/Yellow Two-Tone Swirl
Super Seeds

Ecto

Species: Fancy Banshee
Set: Spookies
Number: 060
Rarity: Rare
Variations: 12

Fancy Banshees may be a bit spooky, but they are also **some of the friendliest Moshlings.** They float around at night, passing through walls and looking for the darkest places to hang out. Their **capes are electrified wobble-plasma** so best not to touch them, or you might find yourself turned **inside out!**

Moshling experts think they come from a parallel vortex deep within the ClothEar Cloud Formation, and that they need Rox dust in order to keep themselves **floating and glowing.** For some reason they don't like the name "Ichabod" and they especially don't like being upside down. Perhaps because their capes fall off?

What are they like?
Fleeting, spooky, quiet and friendly!

Things to look for:
Wobble-plasma cape, haunting hoodie and cheeky face.

Series One

Classic/Ultimate Collection
Blind Bag/Collectors Pack

Where to find 'em:

Ultra Rare

Glitter Purple
Blind Bag/Collectors Pack

Glitter Orange
Blind Bag/Collectors Pack

Glow-in-the-Dark Ghost White
Halloween/Spooky Egg/ Exclusive 2012

Glow-in-the-Dark Scream Green
Halloween/Spooky Egg/ Exclusive 2012

Ultra Rare

Special Pumpkin Heads
Halloween

Glow-in-the-Dark Voodoo Blue
Halloween/Spooky Egg

Shocking Pink
Moshi Surprise Egg 2012

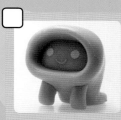

Brilliant Blue
Moshi Surprise Egg 2012

Special Gold
Blind Bag/Collectors Pack

Ultra Rare

Red/Yellow Two-Tone Swirl
Super Seeds

Ultra Rare

Green Two-Tone Swirl
Super Seeds

Gurgle

Species: Performing Flappasaurus
Set: Dinos
Number: 083
Rarity: Ultra Rare
Variations: 14

Not far from the Crazy Canyons there is an **amazing light formation** called the Cadabra Flash. It's here you'll find the Performing Flappasauruses. They love the glow of the Cadabra Flash as much as they adore the glare of publicity, because these little leathery Moshlings are **hungry for fame.**

They love **entertaining with their magic shows** and performing tricks. Like most showbiz types, they're quite sensitive, though. If their performances go wrong, the Performing Flappasauruses are likely to **burst into tears and toast their props** with their fiery breath! Other inhabitants of Monstro City generally applaud politely and wear **flame-proof trousers.**

What are they like?
Limelight-loving, magical and smoky!

Things to look for:
Leathery wings, spiked tail, horned head and googly eyes.

Ultra Rare

Classic/Ultimate Collection
Blind Bag/Collectors Pack

Where to find 'em:

Ultra Rare

Glitter Purple
Blind Bag/Collectors Pack

Glitter Orange
Blind Bag/Collectors Pack

Special Gold
Blind Bag/Collectors Pack/
Collector Tin 1

Glow-in-the-Dark Scream Green
Halloween/Spooky Egg

Glow-in-the-Dark Voodoo Blue
Halloween/Spooky Egg

Glow-in-the-Dark Ghost White
Halloween/Spooky Egg

Ultra Rare

Special Pumpkin Heads
Halloween

Brilliant Blue
Moshi Surprise Egg 2012

Shocking Pink
Moshi Surprise Egg 2012

Red/Yellow Two-Tone Swirl
Super Seeds

Ultra Rare

Ultra Rare

Green Two-Tone Swirl
Super Seeds

Ultra Rare

Goo Green
Moshi Goo

ordering it!

Ultra Rare

Limited Edition Goshi Moshi Blue
Goshi Moshi Tin

Scamp

Species: Froggie Doggie
Set: Puppies
Number: 084
Rarity: Ultra Rare
Variations: 12

✓

> **Things to look for:**
> Pretty bow, cute smile and Froggie costume.

Moshlings can be **strange creatures** and none more so than the Froggie Doggies. They are dogs who like to **dress up as frogs.** Hmmm. Naturally, they hang out at Lillypad Lake and Croak Creek, where they leap about calling out, **"Ribbit! Ribbit!".**

The worst thing that can happen to a Froggie Doggie is to fall in the water, because they **can't swim!** These pad-hopping pooches also dislike people messing with their bows because this deflates their **bizarre bouncy outfits.** This may also explain why they fear knitting needles so much!

Ultra Rare

> **What are they like?**
> Inflatable, bouncy and ribbity!

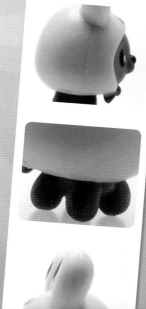

Classic/Ultimate Collection
Blind Bag Collectors Pack

Where to find 'em:

Ultra Rare

Glitter Purple
Blind Bag/Collectors Pack

Glitter Orange
Blind Bag/Collectors Pack

Ultra Rare

Special Pumpkin Heads
Halloween

Glow-in-the-Dark Scream Green
Halloween/Spooky Egg

Glow-in-the-Dark Voodoo Blue
Halloween/Spooky Egg

Glow-in-the-Dark Ghost White
Halloween/Spooky Egg

Ultra Rare

Ultra Rare

Red/Yellow Two-Tone Swirl
Super Seeds

Green Two-Tone Swirl
Super Seeds

Brilliant Blue
Moshi Surprise Egg 2012

Special Gold
Blind Bag

Shocking Pink
Moshi Surprise Egg 2012

General Fuzuki

Species: Warrior Wombat
Set: Ninjas
Number: 082
Rarity: Ultra Rare
Variations: 13

The Warrior Wombats have a proud tradition of guarding all sorts of **intergalactic shiny stuff.** Some think it's because they're fearless, but actually it's because they just don't fall asleep! Or at least that's what Moshlings experts used to think . . .

Researchers observing the Warrior Wombats in their natural habitat of ChillyBot State Park have now realized that what they thought were the Moshlings' ever-open eyes are actually **cake tins welded to their funny Ninja headgear!** So they probably do sleep, but you won't know when. This may explain their love of comfy cushions and **dislike of alarm clocks!**

Ultra Rare

What are they like?
Mysterious, serious and reliable.

Things to look for:
Cake tin eyes, Samurai sword and warrior hat.

Classic/Ultimate Collection
Blind Bag/Collectors Pack

Where to find 'em:

☐
Ultra Rare

Glitter Purple
Blind Bag/Collectors Pack

☐

Glitter Orange
Blind Bag/Collectors Pack

☐

Glow-in-the-Dark Ghost White
Halloween/Spooky Egg

☐

Glow-in-the-Dark Scream Green
Halloween/Spooky Egg

☐

Glow-in-the-Dark Voodoo Blue
Halloween/Spooky Egg

☐
Ultra Rare

Special Pumpkin Heads
Halloween

☑

Shocking Pink
Moshi Surprise Egg 2012

☐

Brilliant Blue
Moshi Surprise Egg 2012

Ultra Rare
☐

Green Two-Tone Swirl
Super Seeds

☐
Special Gold
Blind Bag

Ultra Rare
☐
Red/Yellow Two-Tone Swirl
Super Seeds

☐
Rox Collection 2
Rox Tin 2013

Chop Chop

Things to look for:
Ninja headband, looping tail and primate nose!

What are they like?
Cheeky, mischievous and naughty!

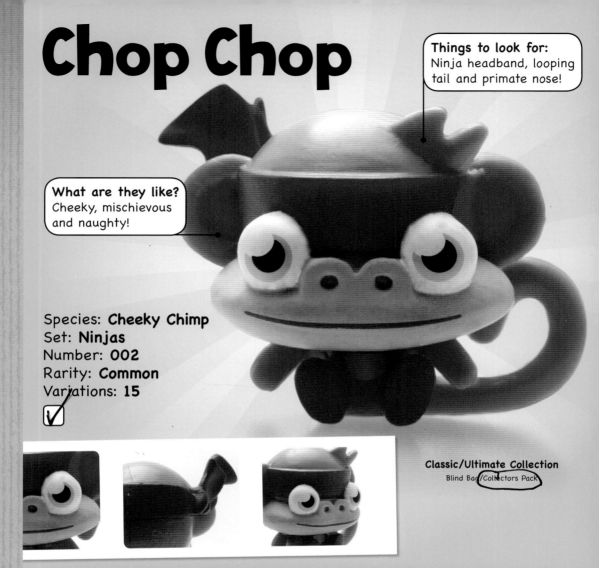

Species: Cheeky Chimp
Set: Ninjas
Number: 002
Rarity: Common
Variations: 15

☑

Classic/Ultimate Collection
Blind Bag/Collectors Pack

Series One

56

Sniggerton Wood is where the Cheeky Chimps practise their ninja moves and not-so ninja jokes. These cheerful chaps are **jolly jesters** and like nothing more than playing **tricks on unsuspecting targets!** Watch your chair when there's a Cheeky Chimp around, as you might find yourself seated on a whoopee cushion or with your shoelaces tied together.

Experts can track this monkey mayhem by following the trail of itching powder, banana skins and stink bombs. The trouble is, Cheeky Chimps **just can't help themselves** when it comes to practical jokes. As far as they're concerned, the more custard pies and rubber chickens their life involves, the better!

Where to find 'em:

Ultra Rare

Glitter Purple
Blind Bag/Collectors Pack

Glitter Orange
Blind Bag/Collectors Pack

Ultra Rare

Special Pumpkin Heads
Halloween

Glow-in-the-Dark Scream Green
Halloween

Glow-in-the-Dark Voodoo Blue
Halloween

Glow-in-the-Dark Ghost White
Halloween

Frostbite Blue
Winter Wonderland

Ultra Rare

Bauble Red
Winter Wonderland

Special Gold
Blind Bag/Collectors Pack/ Collector Tin 1

Electric Yellow
Moshi Surprise Egg 2012

Sonic Orange
Moshi Surprise Egg 2012

Christmas Tree Green
Winter Wonderland

Brilliant Blue
Moshi Surprise Egg 2012

Shocking Pink
Moshi Surprise Egg 2012

Gingersnap

Species: **Whinger Cat**
Set: **Kitties**
Number: **003**
Rarity: **Common**
Variations: **15**

☑

What are they like?
Lazy, cranky and doubtful!

Moan, moan, moan. That's what Whinger Cats are really good at. That, and eating cheese. They like nothing better than **lazing around** and will only really get up to eat. And once they're awake, they'll probably be complaining that they're not asleep.

Their two favourite times of the day are mealtime and bedtime, although they can **eat or sleep anytime** if given the opportunity. They can be found chilling near Hopeless Hill in the Sloth Swamp. Despite being **total layabouts,** they are **very charming** in an effortless kind of way. Just don't ask them to do any work!

Things to look for:
Jaunty cap, scar, sticky-out tongue and zigzag tail.

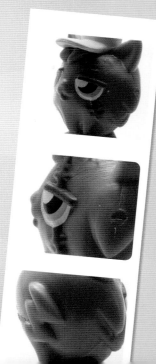

Series One

Classic
Blind Bag/Collectors Pack

Where to find 'em:

Glitter Purple
Blind Bag/Collectors Pack

Ultra Rare

Glitter Orange
Blind Bag/Collectors Pack

Ultra Rare

Special Pumpkin Heads
Halloween

**Glow-in-the-Dark
Scream Green**
Halloween

**Glow-in-the-Dark
Voodoo Blue**
Halloween

**Glow-in-the-Dark
Ghost White**
Halloween

Frostbite Blue
Winter Wonderland

Ultra Rare

Bauble Red
Winter Wonderland

Sonic Orange
Moshi Surprise Egg 2012

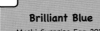

Brilliant Blue
Moshi Surprise Egg 2012

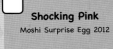

Shocking Pink
Moshi Surprise Egg 2012

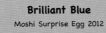

Special Gold
Blind Bag/Collectors Pack/
Collector Tin 1

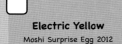

Electric Yellow
Moshi Surprise Egg 2012

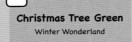

Christmas Tree Green
Winter Wonderland

59

McNulty

Species: Undercover YapYap
Set: Puppies
Number: 038
Rarity: Uncommon
Variations: 18

When it comes to **sniffing out top secrets,** there are no better Moshlings than the Undercover YapYaps. Originally from Sherlock Nook, not far from Waggytail Hollow, these detective doggies now like to hang out in other Moshling neighbourhoods, usually **rummaging through other Moshis' drawers!**

It's difficult to spot them, though, because Undercover YapYaps are **very good at disguising themselves.** The only giveaway to their true identities is their tails, which are always wagging!

What are they like?
Independent, loyal and furtive.

Things to look for:
Tiny, waggy tail and cute puppy dog eyes.

Classic
Blind Bag/Collectors Pack

Where to find 'em:

☐

Ultra Rare

Glitter Purple
Blind Bag/Collectors Pack

☐

Glitter Orange
Blind Bag/Collectors Pack

☐

Special Gold
Blind Bag/Collectors Pack/
Collector Tin 1

☐

Glow-in-the-Dark
Scream Green
Halloween

☐

Glow-in-the-Dark
Voodoo Blue
Halloween

☐

Glow-in-the-Dark
Ghost White
Halloween

☐

Ultra Rare

Special
Pumpkin Heads
Halloween

☐

Ultra Rare

Limited Edition
Goshi Moshi Blue
Goshi Moshi Tin

☐

Ultra Rare

Goo Green
Moshi Goo

✓

Frostbite Blue
~~Winter Wonderland~~

☐

Ultra Rare

Bauble Red
Winter Wonderland

☐

Sonic Orange
Moshi Surprise Egg 2012

☐

Rox Collection 2
Rox Tin 2013

☐

Brilliant Blue
Moshi Surprise Egg 2012

☐

Christmas Tree Green
Winter Wonderland

☐

Electric Yellow
Moshi Surprise Egg 2012

☐

Shocking Pink
Moshi Surprise Egg 2012

Waldo

Species: Tabby Nerdicat
Set: Kitties
Number: 077
Rarity: Rare
Variations: 15

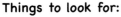

Things to look for:
Speccy eyes, toothy smile, computer pad and tabby tail.

What are they like?
Techy, inventive and super-clever.

Classic
Blind Bag/Collectors Pack

If you're looking for the **geekiest Moshlings**, it's hard to beat the Tabby Nerdicats. These freaky felines are into **comic books and computers.** They can calculate the maddest mathematical formulae, but when it comes to being cool, these cats are a catastrophe. **Don't ever ask them to dance** unless you've secured all breakable objects!

Tabby Nerdicats live in the cubbyholes by the grassy knoll on Honeycomb Hill. They're **rarely seen** because they're usually **hard at work behind closed doors**, fiddling with circuit boards and sharing superhero stories with their geeky friends!

Where to find 'em:

☐
Ultra Rare
Glitter Purple
Blind Bag/Collectors Pack

☐
Glitter Orange
Blind Bag/Collectors Pack

☐
Ultra Rare
Bauble Red
Winter Wonderland

☐
Glow-in-the-Dark Scream Green
Halloween

☐
Glow-in-the-Dark Voodoo Blue
Halloween

☐
Glow-in-the-Dark Ghost White
Halloween

☐
Ultra Rare
Special Pumpkin Heads
Halloween

☐ **Special Gold**
Blind Bag/Collectors Pack/ Collector Tin 1

☐
Electric Yellow
Moshi Surprise Egg 2013

☐ **Brilliant Blue**
Moshi Surprise Egg 2012

☐ **Sonic Orange**
Moshi Surprise Egg 2012

☐ **Shocking Pink**
Moshi Surprise Egg 2012

☐ **Christmas Tree Green**
Winter Wonderland

☑
Frostbite Blue
Winter Wonderland

Fumble

Species: **Acrobatic SeaStar**
Set: **Fishies**
Number: **053**
Rarity: **Rare**
Variations: **17**

These **energetic Moshlings** can be found amongst the coral reefs of Bleurgh Lagoon, or gathered on the beach showing off their moves. Acrobatic SeaStars **love gymnastics,** performing star jumps and slightly more **death-defying stunts.**

The trouble is that they may be **energetic and brave,** but they're also some of the clumsiest sea creatures, so they're often to be found **gluing their pointy bits back on!** If only they could stop showing off, they might spend a lot less Rox on sea gluecumber and sticking plasters.

Things to look for:
Big fishy smile and five pointy limbs!

What are they like?
Rugged, clumsy, fearless and lively.

Classic
Blind Bag/Collectors Pack

Where to find 'em:

Glitter Purple
Ultra Rare
Blind Bag/Collectors Pack

Glitter Orange
Blind Bag/Collectors Pack

Special Gold
Blind Bag/Collectors Pack/
Collector Tin 1

Glow-in-the-Dark
Voodoo Blue
Halloween

Glow-in-the-Dark
Scream Green
Halloween

Goo Green
Ultra Rare
Moshi Goo

Frostbite Blue
Winter Wonderland

Bauble Red
Ultra Rare
Winter Wonderland

Special
Pumpkin Heads
Ultra Rare
Halloween

Brilliant Blue
Moshi Surprise Egg 2012

Sonic Orange
Moshi Surprise Egg 2012

Limited Edition
Goshi Moshi Blue
Ultra Rare
Goshi Moshi Tin

Electric Yellow
Moshi Surprise Egg 2012

Shocking Pink
Moshi Surprise Egg 2012

Glow-in-the-Dark
Ghost White
Halloween

Christmas Tree Green
Winter Wonderland

Hansel

Species: **Pyscho Gingerboy**
Set: **Foodies**
Number: **059**
Rarity: **Rare**
Variations: **16**

What are they like?
Disobedient, sugary and rascally.

Things to look for:
Frosted sleeves and trousers, candy buttons and big, mad eyes!

Classic
Blind Bag/Collectors Pack

These **biscuity bad boys** were cooked up deep inside Cookie Crumb Canyon, but since then the Psycho Gingerboys have spread everywhere. Now, these critters may look **cute and yummy** with their fancy frosting and plump raisins, **but they're anything but!**

When they're not pilfering pancakes and stealing sweeties, they can be found **holding-up bakeries** or loitering on the street corners of Monstro City, tripping up passers-by with their candy canes. Luckily, Psycho Gingerboys are **easy to catch,** as they always leave a trail of gingerbread crumbs!

Series One

Where to find 'em:

Glitter Purple
Blind Bag/Collectors Pack

Ultra Rare

Glitter Orange
Blind Bag/Collectors Pack

Glow-in-the-Dark Voodoo Blue
Halloween

Glow-in-the-Dark Scream Green
Halloween

Frostbite Blue
Winter Wonderland

Ultra Rare

Special Pumpkin Heads
Halloween

Bauble Red
Winter Wonderland

Ultra Rare

No Longer Available

Glitter Red Moshi Magazine Exclusive
Covermount for Issue 11

Glow-in-the-Dark Ghost White
Halloween

Electric Yellow
Moshi Surprise Egg 2012

Shocking Pink
Moshi Surprise Egg 2012

Special Gold
Blind Bag/Collectors Pack/
Collector Tin 1

Sonic Orange
Moshi Surprise Egg 2012

Brilliant Blue
Moshi Surprise Egg 2012

Christmas Tree Green
Winter Wonderland

Burnie

Species: **Fiery Frazzledragon**
Set: **Beasties**
Number: **078**
Rarity: **Ultra Rare**
Variations: **16**

If you want to make friends with these **cheeky flying Beasties**, try taking them an ash-flavoured hot cake, as it's the Fiery Frazzledragon's favourite treat! They guzzle them down with a **gallon or two of gasoline**, which gives them **terrible flaming hiccups**, so stand back! Whatever you do, don't bring a fire extinguisher though, as Fiery Frazzledragons hate them!

These cute dragons can be found **flapping around Mount CharChar**, on the volcanic island of Emberooze. You might also find them at **Super Moshi HQ**, where they have been known to heat up cauldrons of dew stew and char-grill Silly Sausages.

What are they like?
Cheeky and too hot to handle!

Things to look for:
Hot horns, smoking nostrils, pointy tail and fluttery wings.

Ultra Rare

Classic
Blind Bag/Collectors Pack/Zoo 2012

Where to find 'em:

☐
Glitter Purple
Blind Bag/Collectors Pack

☐
Glitter Orange
Blind Bag/Collectors Pack

☐
Glow-in-the-Dark Ghost White
Halloween

☐
Glow-in-the-Dark Scream Green
Halloween

☑
Glow-in-the-Dark Voodoo Blue
Halloween

☐
Bauble Red
Winter Wonderland

☐
Special Pumpkin Heads
Halloween

☒
Frostbite Blue
~~Winter Wonderland~~

☐ **Brilliant Blue**
Moshi Surprise Egg 2012

☐ **Sonic Orange**
Moshi Surprise Egg 2012

☑ **Christmas Tree Green**
Winter Wonderland

☐ **Rox Collection 2**
Rox Tin 2013

☐ **Shocking Pink**
Moshi Surprise Egg 2012

☐ **Electric Yellow**
Moshi Surprise Egg 2012

☐ **Special Gold**
Blind Bag/Collectors Pack/
Collector Tin 1

69

Cutie Pie

Species: Wheelie YumYum
Set: Foodies
Number: 091
Rarity: Ultra Rare
Variations: 15

Things to look for:
Flashing cherry, delicious sprinkles and four-wheel drive!

Ultra Rare

What are they like?
Fast, four-wheeled, sociable and quick off the mark!

Classic
Blind Bag/Collectors Pack/Zoo 2012

No Moshlings live up to their name as much as the Wheelie YumYums. They **zip about at top speed**, with their cherries flashing. No one knows exactly where they come from, apart from the fact it's called CutiePie Canyon. If you travel to Ramekin Plain, you can smell a **lovely cakey aroma,** so it may be near there!

It's good that these tasty treats can move so fast as they often have to **evade hungry cake-lovers.** The only time they slow down is to fill up on premium high-grade, super-sweet cocoa. They love all hot drinks, but cocoa is their fave!

Where to find 'em:

Ultra Rare

Glitter Purple
Blind Bag/Collectors Pack

Glitter Orange
Blind Bag/Collectors Pack

Frostbite Blue
Winter Wonderland

Glow-in-the-Dark Scream Green
Halloween

Glow-in-the-Dark Voodoo Blue
Halloween

Glow-in-the-Dark Ghost White
Halloween

Ultra Rare

Special Pumpkin Heads
Halloween

Special Gold
Blind Bag/Collectors Pack/ Collector Tin 1

Sonic Orange
Moshi Surprise Egg 2012

Ultra Rare

Bauble Red
Winter Wonderland

Brilliant Blue
Moshi Surprise Egg 2012

Shocking Pink
Moshi Surprise Egg 2012

Electric Yellow
Moshi Surprise Egg 2012

Christmas Tree Green
Winter Wonderland

71

FiFi

Species: **Oochie Poochie**
Set: **Puppies**
Number: **007**
Rarity: **Common**
Variations: **18**

What are they like?
Posh, fashionable and pushy!

Things to look for:
Heart hair clip, fluffy ears, flossy tail and adorable nose.

Oochie Poochies are seen in all the right places, darling! That's because they are the **most fashionable trend-setters.** They love to read *Dogue* magazine to see what the latest fur-styles are, and then **rush out to the stylist** to get the latest looks.

Naturally these Puppies are used to the **finer things in life,** such as vintage pink lemonade and choco-caviar. Their **passion for poshness** means that they're also keen on ironed napkins and perfect manners. But if they get peckish and aren't near a five star restaurant, they can always **nibble at their candyfloss tails!**

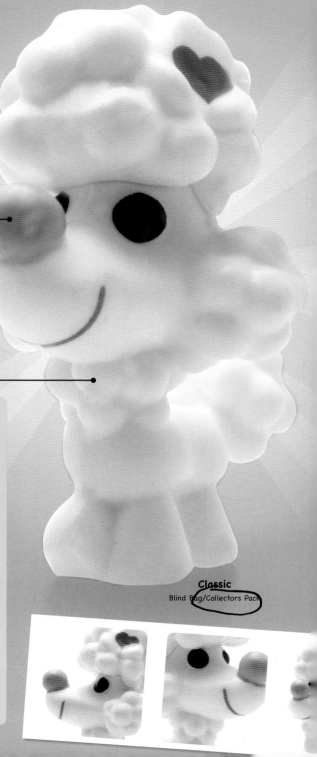

Classic
Blind Bag/Collectors Pack

Where to find 'em:

Ultra Rare

Glitter Purple
Blind Bag/Collectors Pack

Glitter Orange
Blind Bag/Collectors Pack

Special Gold
Blind Bag/Collectors Pack/
Collector Tin 2

Glow-in-the-Dark Scream Green
Halloween

Glow-in-the-Dark Voodoo Blue
Halloween

Glow-in-the-Dark Ghost White
Halloween

Special Pumpkin Heads
Halloween

Ultra Rare

Frostbite Blue
Winter Wonderland/
Advent Calender

Ultra Rare

Red/Yellow Two-Tone Swirl
Super Seeds

Green Two-Tone Swirl
Super Seeds

Ultra Rare

Ultra Rare

Bauble Red
Winter Wonderland

No Longer Available

Glitter Red Moshi Magazine Exclusive
Covermount for Issue 11

Brilliant Blue
Moshi Surprise Egg 2012

Shocking Pink
Moshi Surprise Egg 2012

Sonic Orange
Moshi Surprise Egg 2012

Electric Yellow
Moshi Surprise Egg 2012

Christmas Tree Green
Winter Wonderland

Kissy

What are they like?
Endearing, fragile, flirty and shy.

Species: **Baby Ghost**
Set: **Spookies**
Number: **027**
Rarity: **Uncommon**
Variations: **17**

Things to look for:
Tiny feet, big smile, hugging arms and cute little bow.

Classic
Blind Bag/Collectors Pack

Baby Ghosts **would love to scare everyone** but they're so lovely they **simply can't do it!** So these supernatural Moshlings turn their attention to making themselves even more darling with tutus, cute booties, false eyelashes, bows and ribbons!

These **charming ghosties** pop out of the plasma clouds, high above the abandoned Harem Scarum pickling plant in the Okay-ish Lands. They love loganberry lip gloss and fluffy poodles, but if you breathe on one they might **evaporate in a puff of pink air,** leaving behind nothing but their itsy-bitsy fashion accessories.

Where to find 'em:

Ultra Rare

Glitter Purple
Blind Bag/Collectors Pack

Glitter Orange
Blind Bag/Collectors Pack

✓

Ultra Rare

Bauble Red
Winter Wonderland

Glow-in-the-Dark Scream Green
Halloween

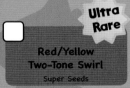

Glow-in-the-Dark Voodoo Blue
Halloween

Glow-in-the-Dark Ghost White
Halloween

Special Pumpkin Heads
Halloween

✓

Ultra Rare

Frostbite Blue
Winter Wonderland/ Advent Calender

Ultra Rare

Red/Yellow Two-Tone Swirl
Super Seeds

Ultra Rare

Green Two-Tone Swirl
Super Seeds

Sonic Orange
Moshi Surprise Egg 2012

Electric Yellow
Moshi Surprise Egg 2012

Christmas Tree Green
Winter Wonderland

Brilliant Blue
Moshi Surprise Egg 2012

Shocking Pink
Moshi Surprise Egg 2012

Special Gold
Blind Bag/Collectors Pack

Lady Meowford

Species: Pretty Kitty
Set: Kitties
Number: 030
Rarity: Uncommon
Variations: 17

What are they like?
Intelligent, sophisticated and snobbish.

Things to look for:
Pretty little dress, amazing eyelashes and elegant tail.

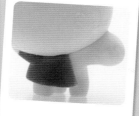

Classic
Blind Bag Collectors Pack

Pretty Kitties are **frightfully sweet but a bit annoying.** They are also **always right.** About everything. They live their superior lives way up in the High and Mighty Mountains, as everywhere else is beneath them. Being so pretty, sweet and clever, these Moshlings can sometimes come across as a bit snooty.

They love classical music and have **incredibly high-pitched singing voices.** They are also fluent in loads of languages, ski like Olympic champions, and are **excellent lacrosse players.** When they're not skiing or chatting to foreign dignitaries, Pretty Kitties relax by dipping into a box of toffee-nosed plums.

Where to find 'em:

Ultra Rare

Glitter Purple
Blind Bag/Collectors Pack

Glitter Orange
Blind Bag/Collectors Pack

 ✓

Frostbite Blue
Winter Wonderland/
Advent Calender

**Glow-in-the-Dark
Scream Green**
Halloween

**Glow-in-the-Dark
Voodoo Blue**
Halloween

**Glow-in-the-Dark
Ghost White**
Halloween

Ultra Rare

**Special
Pumpkin Heads**
Halloween

Ultra Rare

Bauble Red
Winter Wonderland

Sonic Orange
Moshi Surprise Egg 2012

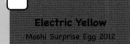

Electric Yellow
Moshi Surprise Egg 2012

Brilliant Blue
Moshi Surprise Egg 2012

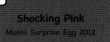

Shocking Pink
Moshi Surprise Egg 2012

Ultra Rare

**Red/Yellow
Two-Tone Swirl**
Super Seeds

Ultra Rare

Green Two-Tone Swirl
Super Seeds

Special Gold
Blind Bag/Collectors Pack

✓

Christmas Tree Green
Winter Wonderland

Dipsy

Species: **Dinky Dreamcloud**
Set: **Fluffies**
Number: **034**
Rarity: **Uncommon**
Variations: **17**

☑

Although **fluffy and adorable**, Dinky Dreamclouds aspire to be much bigger, Ginormous Dreamclouds. They live in Meringue Meadow, surrounded by towering vanilla pod trees and wild candyfloss. Here, they **float about all day** making cute noises and admiring their eyelashes.

If Dinky Dreamclouds become angry, they can turn very thundery, **blasting bolts of lightning** in all directions and raining on whoever has upset them, **so be warned!**

What are they like?
Cheery, bright, unpredictable and whimsical.

Things to look for:
Fluffy body, wonderful eyelashes and doe eyes.

Classic
Blind Bag/Collectors Pack

Where to find 'em:

Ultra Rare

Glitter Purple
Blind Bag/Collectors Pack

Glitter Orange
Blind Bag/Collectors Pack

✓

Frostbite Blue
~~Winter Wonderland/~~
~~Advent Calendar~~

Glow-in-the-Dark Scream Green
Halloween

Glow-in-the-Dark Voodoo Blue
Halloween

Glow-in-the-Dark Ghost White
Halloween

Ultra Rare

Bauble Red
Winter Wonderland

Ultra Rare

Special Pumpkin Heads
Halloween

Ultra Rare

Green Two-Tone Swirl
Super Seeds

Ultra Rare

Red/Yellow Two-Tone Swirl
Super Seeds

Brilliant Blue
Moshi Surprise Egg 2012

Shocking Pink
Moshi Surprise Egg 2012

Sonic Orange
Moshi Surprise Egg 2012

Electric Yellow
Moshi Surprise Egg 2012

Special Gold
Blind Bag/Collectors Pack

✓

Christmas Tree Green
~~Winter Wonderland~~

Funny Bunnies are **seriously trendy**, so you wouldn't find these hip hoppers living in basic burrows. Oh no! Most of them have **state-of-the art hutches** in Pawberry Fields. When not relaxing at home, they're often out and about **texting jokes** to one another, or chatting about the latest styles of carrot cake, clothes and fur straighteners!

Of course, the one thing they can never completely straighten is their floppy ear, believed to be caused by spending so much time **listening to silly ringtones!**

Honey

Species: **Funny Bunny**
Set: **Fluffies**
Number: **057**
Rarity: **Rare**
Variations: **17**

What are they like?
Confident, fashionable and chatty.

Things to look for:
Spotty top, floppy ear, pretty freckles and stumpy whiskers.

Classic
Blind Bag/Collectors Pack

Where to find 'em:

Ultra Rare

Glitter Purple
Blind Bag/Collectors Pack

Glitter Orange
Blind Bag/Collectors Pack

Special Gold
Blind Bag/Collectors Pack/
Collector Tin 2

**Glow-in-the-Dark
Voodoo Blue**
Halloween

**Glow-in-the-Dark
Ghost White**
Halloween

Ultra Rare

Green Two-Tone Swirl
Super Seeds

Ultra Rare

**Red/Yellow
Two-Tone Swirl**
Super Seeds

Frostbite Blue
Winter Wonderland/
Advent Calender

Ultra Rare

**Special
Pumpkin Heads**
Halloween

**Glow-in-the-Dark
Scream Green**
Halloween

Brilliant Blue
Moshi Surprise Egg 2012

Shocking Pink
Moshi Surprise Egg 2012

Ultra Rare

Bauble Red
Winter Wonderland

Sonic Orange
Moshi Surprise Egg 2012

Electric Yellow
Moshi Surprise Egg 2012

Christmas Tree Green
Winter Wonderland

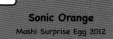

White Fang

Species: Musky Husky
Set: Puppies
Number: 055
Rarity: Rare
Variations: 17

What are they like?
Ravenous, scruffy, wild and slightly dangerous.

Things to look for:
Rugged tail, panting tongue and mad eyes.

Classic
Blind Bag/Collectors Pack

Musky Huskies are famous all over Monstro City as one of their kind **bit off the hand of the terrible Dr. Strangeglove.** They're truly wild and don't live in any one place, preferring to **roam the streets** checking out dumpsters for scraps of food, doggie bags and old bones.

Musky Huskies are **unpredictable and considered a bit barking!** They also pong a bit – probably because they're **always raiding bins.** The one thing they can't stand, though, is getting tin cans stuck on their noses – which is a real danger when sticking their snouts in dustbins!

Where to find 'em:

Glitter Purple
Blind Bag/Collectors Pack

Ultra Rare

Glitter Orange
Blind Bag/Collectors Pack

Frostbite Blue
Winter Wonderland/
Advent Calender

**Glow-in-the-Dark
Scream Green**
Halloween

**Glow-in-the-Dark
Voodoo Blue**
Halloween

**Glow-in-the-Dark
Ghost White**
Halloween

Ultra Rare

Special Pumpkin Heads
Halloween

Ultra Rare

Bauble Red
Winter Wonderland

Special Gold
Blind Bag/Collectors Pack

Ultra Rare

**Red/Yellow
Two-Tone Swirl**
Super Seeds

Christmas Tree Green
Winter Wonderland

Ultra Rare

Brilliant Blue
Moshi Surprise Egg 2012

Green Two-Tone Swirl
Super Seeds

Sonic Orange
Moshi Surprise Egg 2012

Shocking Pink
Moshi Surprise Egg 2012

Electric Yellow
Moshi Surprise Egg 2012

Peppy

Species: **Stunt Penguin**
Set: **Birdies**
Number: **071**
Rarity: **Rare**
Variations: **18**

Stunt Penguins are **obsessed with anything with two wheels** – especially motorbikes. Trouble is, they're **too small to ride them** as their feet don't reach the pedals! Instead, they happily slide along the ground making motorcycle noises and **pretending to rev their engines.**

These **helmeted half-pints** live on the Frosty Pop Glacier, a wintry wonderland near Potion Ocean. They love it there because they can **feast on pilchard popsicles** – often eating more than 100 a day! You might be able to smell these Moshlings coming because they tend to store the pilchard pops under their crash helmets for a **quick snack when they're peckish.**

Things to look for:
Goggles and helmet with skull and crossbones.

What are they like?
Reckless, rebellious, and wheel-obsessed.

Classic
Blind Bag Collectors Pack

Where to find 'em:

Ultra Rare

Glitter Purple
Blind Bag/Collectors Pack

Glitter Orange
Blind Bag/Collectors Pack

Ultra Rare

Special Pumpkin Heads
Halloween

Glow-in-the-Dark Scream Green
Halloween

Glow-in-the-Dark Voodoo Blue
Halloween

Glow-in-the-Dark Ghost White
Halloween

Frostbite Blue
Winter Wonderland/ Advent Calender

Ultra Rare

Bauble Red
Winter Wonderland

Special Gold
Blind Bag/Collectors Pack

Green Two-Tone Swirl
Super Seeds

Ultra Rare

Ultra Rare

Red/Yellow Two-Tone Swirl
Super Seeds

Rox Collection 2
Rox Tin 2013

Sonic Orange
Moshi Surprise Egg 2012

Brilliant Blue
Moshi Surprise Egg 2012

Electric Yellow
Moshi Surprise Egg 2012

Shocking Pink
Moshi Surprise Egg 2012

Christmas Tree Green
Winter Wonderland

Flumpy

Species: **Pluff**
Set: **Fluffies**
Number: **054**
Rarity: **Rare**
Variations: **17**

☑

Pluffs can be found in the Cotton Clump Plantation but they also enjoy **strolling through Monstro City**, smiling at everyone they meet! The most chilled out of all Moshlings, their extra long arms are great for giving **extra big hugs**.

Pluffs are also **very neat and clean** – they can't stand clutter! You'll often find them **donning rubber gloves** in order to give their furniture a good polish, or maybe even using their heads!

What are they like?
Jovial, carefree and big-hearted.

Things to look for:
Long, huggy arms, big smile and fleecy body.

Classic
Blind Bag/Collectors Pack

Series One

Where to find 'em:

Ultra Rare

Bauble Red
Winter Wonderland

Glitter Orange
Blind Bag/Collectors Pack

✓

Frostbite Blue
Winter Wonderland/
Advent Calendar

**Glow-in-the-Dark
Scream Green**
Halloween

**Glow-in-the-Dark
Voodoo Blue**
Halloween

**Glow-in-the-Dark
Ghost White**
Halloween

Ultra Rare

Glitter Purple
Blind Bag/Collectors Pack

Ultra Rare

**Special
Pumpkin Heads**
Halloween

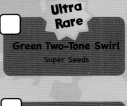

Ultra Rare

Green Two-Tone Swirl
Super Seeds

Special Gold
Blind Bag/Collectors Pack

Brilliant Blue
Moshi Surprise Egg 2012

Shocking Pink
Moshi Surprise Egg 2012

Electric Yellow
Moshi Surprise Egg 2012

✓

Christmas Tree Green
Winter Wonderland

Sonic Orange
Moshi Surprise Egg 2012

**Red/Yellow
Two-Tone Swirl**
Super Seeds

Ultra Rare

ShiShi

Species: Sneezing Panda
Set: Beasties
Number: 087
Rarity: Ultra Rare
Variations: 17

✓

Sneezing Pandas are so called because they **sneeze whenever they watch Monstrovision.** And they watch it a lot! It seems these poor Pandas are **allergic to pixels,** quite the opposite of Pixel-Munching Snafflers who can't get enough of them.

Being big TV watchers, it isn't surprising they come from Gogglebox Gulch, although these **sniffling channel hoppers** will live anywhere as long as they have a big screen to watch and a supply of extra-soft tissues for their noses. They are very **fond of wamwoo shoots,** which they scoff by the bucket load. But hold the pepper, please!

Ultra Rare

What are they like?
Remote, switched on and well informed!

Things to look for:
Goggle-eyes, tummy patch and dish-like ears.

Classic
Blind Bag/Collectors Pack

Where to find 'em:

Glitter Purple
Blind Bag/Collectors Pack

Ultra Rare

Glitter Orange
Blind Bag/Collectors Pack

Special Gold
Blind Bag/Collectors Pack/
Collector Tin 2

**Glow-in-the-Dark
Scream Green**
Halloween

**Glow-in-the-Dark
Voodoo Blue**
Halloween

**Glow-in-the-Dark
Ghost White**
Halloween

**Special
Pumpkin Heads**
Halloween

Ultra Rare

Green Two-Tone Swirl
Super Seeds

Ultra Rare

**Red/Yellow
Two-Tone Swirl**
Super Seeds

Ultra Rare

Frostbite Blue
Winter Wonderland/
Advent Calender

Bauble Red
Winter Wonderland

Ultra Rare

Brilliant Blue
Moshi Surprise Egg 2012

Shocking Pink
Moshi Surprise Egg 2012

Sonic Orange
Moshi Surprise Egg 2012

Electric Yellow
Moshi Surprise Egg 2012

Christmas Tree Green
Winter Wonderland

Gigi

Species: Magical Mule
Set: Ponies
Number: 079
Rarity: Ultra Rare
Variations: 18

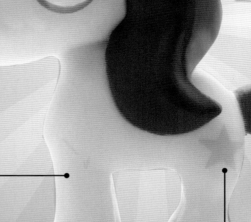

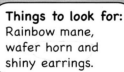

Ultra Rare

What are they like?
Beguiling, charming, graceful and vibrant.

Things to look for:
Rainbow mane, wafer horn and shiny earrings.

Classic
Blind Bag/Collectors Pack

Many people think that Magical Mules look like they **belong on a merry-go-round,** and they may be right because these magical Moshlings are the **descendants of enchanted carousel horses.** That's why they glide up and down **humming fairground music** around the Crystal Grotto near Copperfield Canyon.

Don't be fooled by the "horn" on their heads – these glamorous gee-gees are not related to Lunicorns. Far from it in fact, because those **horns are actually ice cream cones** held on with liquorice shoelaces!

Where to find 'em:

Ultra Rare

Glitter Purple
Blind Bag/Collectors Pack

Glitter Orange
Blind Bag/Collectors Pack

✓

~~Frostbite Blue~~
Winter Wonderland /
Advent Calender

**Glow-in-the-Dark
Scream Green**
Halloween

**Glow-in-the-Dark
Voodoo Blue**
Halloween

**Glow-in-the-Dark
Ghost White**
Halloween

Ultra Rare

**Special
Pumpkin Heads**
Halloween

Ultra Rare

Bauble Red
Winter Wonderland

Special Gold
Blind Bag/Collectors Pack

Electric Yellow
Moshi Surprise Egg 2012

Sonic Orange
Moshi Surprise Egg 2012

Shocking Pink
Moshi Surprise Egg 2012

Green Two-Tone Swirl
Super Seeds

Ultra Rare

Brilliant Blue
Moshi Surprise Egg 2012

Rox Collection 2
Rox Tin 2013

Ultra Rare

**Red/Yellow
Two-Tone Swirl**
Super Seeds

Christmas Tree Green
Winter Wonderland

Snookums

Species: **Baby Tumteedums**
Set: **Dinos**
Number: **010**
Rarity: **Common**
Variations: **10**

What are they like?
Shy, ancient, innocent and needy.

Things to look for:
Dino-spine, ridged tail, small horns and Yuckberry-slurping tongue.

Classic
Blind Bag Collectors Pack

Baby Tumteedums are sweet little demi-dinos that are hatched from **mysterious marzipan eggs.** These Moshlings always need someone to look after them but it's not because they are so young. Quite the opposite, actually: Baby Tumteedums **age in reverse,** so although they look like babies they're actually hundreds of years old!

They particularly **love boiled cabbage** and shuffling around in their carpet slippers, and are often found close to yuckberry bushes, stuffing their faces with the juicy fruit.

Where to find 'em:

Ultra Rare

Glitter Purple
Blind Bag/Collectors Pack

Glitter Orange
Blind Bag/Collectors Pack

Special Gold
Blind Bag/Collectors Pack/
Collector Tin 1

Glow-in-the-Dark
Scream Green
Halloween/Spooky Egg

Glow-in-the-Dark
Voodoo Blue
Halloween/Spooky Egg

Glow-in-the-Dark
Ghost White
Halloween/Spooky Egg

Ultra Rare

Special
Pumpkin Heads
Halloween

Ultra Rare

Limited Edition
Goshi Moshi Blue
Goshi Moshi Tin

Ultra Rare

Goo Green
Moshi Goo

93

Humphrey

Species: **Snoring Hickopotumus**
Set: **Beasties**
Number: **023**
Rarity: **Common**
Variations: **8**

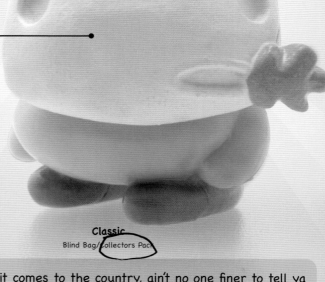

What are they like?
Happy-go-lucky, snoozy and country-bumpkiny.

Things to look for:
Hat, straw and sleepy eyes.

Classic
Blind Bag/Collectors Pack

When it comes to the country, ain't no one finer to tell ya all about it than a Snoring Hickopotumus! These farming Moshlings love nothing better than **digging, sowing, milking and mowing** and generally working the ranch up at Skedaddle Prairie down in **Whoop 'n' Holler Valley!**

Of course if you work hard, you snooze hard, too. And all Snoring Hickopotumuses **enjoy grabbing forty-winks** under the shade of a wacky windmill. They also love playing the banjo and chewing on stalks of enchanted corn.

Where to find 'em:

☐

Ultra Rare

Glitter Purple
Blind Bag/Collectors Pack

☐

Glitter Orange
Blind Bag/Collectors Pack

☐

Glow-in-the-Dark Voodoo Blue
Halloween/Spooky Egg

☐

Glow-in-the-Dark Scream Green
Halloween/Spooky Egg

☐

Glow-in-the-Dark Ghost White
Halloween/Spooky Egg

☐

Ultra Rare

Special Pumpkin Heads
Halloween

☐ **Special Gold**
Blind Bag/Collectors Pack/
Collector Tin 1

Doris

Species: **Rummaging Plotamus**
Set: **Dinos**
Number: **040**
Rarity: **Uncommon**
Variations: **8**

What are they like?
Dozy, nosy, gossipy and fluffle-loving!

Things to look for:
Digging horn, pink bow and dino-spines.

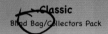

Classic
Blind Bag/Collectors Pack

Rummaging Plotamuses love fluffles: valuable **toadstools that smell of liquorice.** They'll live anywhere their favourite fungi can be found, but Friendly-Tree Woods is a particularly popular hangout. They **dig around for hours** looking for the tasty delicacies, which explains why they're so good at gardening – they are expert diggers.

The **gentle, plodding Moshlings** use the fluffles to knit themselves nests in which they hibernate for up to a year! When they wake up they get straight back to burrowing around, **catching up on the latest celeb gossip** and getting their nails done.

Where to find 'em:

Glitter Orange
Blind Bag/Collectors Pack

Ultra Rare

Ultra Rare

Glitter Purple
Blind Bag/Collectors Pack

Special Pumpkin Heads
Halloween

Glow-in-the-Dark Scream Green
Halloween/Spooky Egg

Glow-in-the-Dark Voodoo Blue
Halloween/Spooky Egg

Glow-in-the-Dark Ghost White
Halloween/Spooky Egg

Special Gold
Blind Bag/Collectors Pack/
Collector Tin 1

97

There's a good reason these Toucans are known as Pilfering: they **can't resist "borrowing" other Moshlings' stuff.** Perhaps this is because they used to sail the seventy seas with the **toughest bunch of salty yuckaneers** that ever lived.

When Moshlings go looking for their stuff, they head for the high palm trees near Lush Lagoon. It's here that Pilfering Toucans **store their stash** in hammocks made of coconut-hair. They love salty gobstoppers, **playing the squeezebox** and drinking punch!

Tiki

Species: **Pilfering Toucan**
Set: **Birdies**
Number: **065**
Rarity: **Rare**
Variations: **8**

✓

What are they like?
Naughty, troublesome and chirpy!

Things to look for:
Colourful beak and wings and loud squawk.

Classic
Blind Bag/Collectors Pack

Where to find 'em:

Glow-in-the-Dark Scream Green
Halloween/Spooky Egg

Glitter Orange
Blind Bag/Collectors Pack

Ultra Rare

Ultra Rare

Special Pumpkin Heads
Halloween

Glitter Purple
Blind Bag/Collectors Pack

Glow-in-the-Dark Voodoo Blue
Halloween/Spooky Egg

Glow-in-the-Dark Ghost White
Halloween/Spooky Egg

Special Gold
Blind Bag/Collectors Pack/ Collector Tin 1

Prof. Purplex

Species: Owl of Wiseness
Set: Birdies
Number: 074
Rarity: Rare
Variations: 8

High in the trees of **Wobbly Woods** lives a very private kind of Moshling – the Owls of Wiseness. They are **solitary birdies** who seldom venture from their nests, possibly because they are **banned from every library** and book shop in the land!

Why are they banned? Because these clever feathered fowl have **a real appetite for knowledge.** Literally! They will eat any book they see, and can **devour an entire encyclopaedia** in ten seconds. The birdy boffins also love comics because pictures are worth a thousand words!

What are they like?
Well-informed, well-read and well-fed!

Classic
Blind Bag/Collectors Pack

Things to look for:
Wise eyes and book-munching beak.

Where to find 'em:

Ultra Rare

Glitter Purple
Blind Bag/Collectors Pack

Glitter Orange
Blind Bag/Collectors Pack

Ultra Rare

Special Pumpkin Heads
Halloween

**Glow-in-the-Dark
Voodoo Blue**
Halloween/Spooky Egg

**Glow-in-the-Dark
Ghost White**
Halloween/Spooky Egg

Glow-in-the-Dark Scream Green
Halloween/Spooky Egg

Special Gold
Blind Bag/Collectors Pack/
Collector Tin 1

Liberty

Species: **Happy Statue**
Set: **Worldies**
Number: **061**
Rarity: **Rare**
Variations: **9**

Things to look for:
Spiky wish crown, star-spangled ice cream, wish list and heart headband.

What are they like?
Brash, self-assured and cheery.

Classic
Blind Bag/Collectors Pack

Happy Statues can be found on Divinity Island but rumour has it that they come from a **mysterious land called Prance.** In one hand they always carry a star-spangled ice cream, and in the other, a **never-ending wish list** because these Moshlings believe in having fun!

It's said that every time Happy Statues think of a new wish, **their crowns light up.** They aren't spoiled, it's just that they love to dream about all the **things they like best in the world:** delicious treats, cool clothes, sparkling trinkets and especially Big Apples!

Where to find 'em:

Glitter Purple
Blind Bag/Collectors Pack

Ultra Rare

Glitter Orange
Blind Bag/Collectors Pack

Glow-in-the-Dark Scream Green
Halloween/Spooky Egg

Glow-in-the-Dark Voodoo Blue
Halloween/Spooky Egg

Glow-in-the-Dark Ghost White
Halloween/Spooky Egg

Special Pumpkin Heads
Halloween

Ultra Rare

Rox Collection 1
Rox Tin 2012

Special Gold
Blind Bag/Collectors Pack/
Collector Tin 1

Big Bad Bill

Species: **Woolly Blue Hoodoo**
Set: **Spookies**
Number: **089**
Rarity: **Ultra Rare**
Variations: **9**

☑

Ultra Rare

Things to look for:
Eyepatch, skull-topped Staff of Power and pointy ears.

Classic
Blind Bag/Collectors Pack/Zoo 2012

What are they like?
Wise, mystical and generous.

Woolly Blue Hoodoos are rarely seen without their **mystical Staves of Power.** Maybe the power is healing, because these wise old Moshlings know everything there is to know about **lotions, potions, hexes and spells.**

Woolly Blue Hoodoos are nomadic and wander vast areas **in search of enlightenment and Oobla Doobla.** It's said that they come from a lost tribe found deep in the Gombala Gombala Jungle. Just don't go near them with a teaspoon or a clown . . . Both of these will make the **funny little furballs** head for the hills!

Where to find 'em:

Glow-in-the-Dark Scream Green
Halloween/Spooky Egg

Glitter Orange
Blind Bag/Collectors Pack

Glow-in-the-Dark Ghost White
Halloween/Spooky Egg

Ultra Rare

Special Pumpkin Heads
Halloween

Glow-in-the-Dark Voodoo Blue
Halloween/Spooky Egg

No Longer Available

Glitter Red Moshi Magazine Exclusive
Covermount for Issue 11

Special Gold
Blind Bag/Collectors Pack/ Collector Tin 1

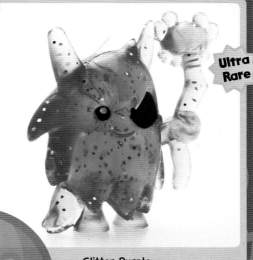

Ultra Rare

Glitter Purple
Blind Bag/Collectors Pack

Cherry Bomb

Species: **Baby Boomer**
Set: **Noisies**
Number: **075**
Rarity: **Rare**
Variations: **9**

☑

What are they like?
Fizzy, unpredictable, bombastic and loud.

Things to look for:
Short fuse and round body.

Not surprisingly, a Baby Boomer's favourite food is **bangers and crash with dynamite sauce.** They chow down on this in Kaboom Canyon, but can pop up anywhere, with their **fuses fizzing** away.

There's **no cause for panic** though. They might be noisy but they don't explode very often! All that din is just their fuses **fizzing and crackling** when they get excited!

Where to find 'em:

Classic
Blind Bag/Collectors Pack

☐

Special Gold
Blind Bag/Collectors Pack

☐ **Brilliant Blue**
Moshi Surprise Egg 2012

☐ **Shocking Pink**
Moshi Surprise Egg 2012

☐ **Electric Yellow**
Moshi Surprise Egg 2012

☐ **Sonic Orange**
Moshi Surprise Egg 2012

Ultra Rare
Glitter Green
Blind Bag/Collectors Pack

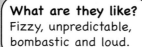

Glitter Yellow
Blind Bag/Collectors Pack

☑ Ultra Rare
Twistmas Edition
Advent Calendar

Tiamo

Sparkly Sweethearts are **magical Moshlings** who appear out of nowhere to help others in distress with their **sparkling energy auras.** No one knows for sure where they come from but you can sometimes hear their **rhythmic pulsing** near Blisskiss Valley.

When these hearty Smilies aren't performing life-saving magic and **helping the needy,** they love d-dumfing to the musical beat of power ballads. They always eat their **five a day,** but they aren't so keen on egg yolks.

Species: Sparkly Sweetheart
Set: Smilies
Number: 032
Rarity: Uncommon
Variations: 8

What are they like?
Helpful, gracious and sparkly.

Things to look for:
All heart!

Where to find 'em:

Classic
Blind Bag/Collectors Pack

Ultra Rare
Glitter Green
Blind Bag/Collectors Pack

Glitter Yellow
Blind Bag/Collectors Pack

Special Gold
Blind Bag/Collectors Pack

Brilliant Blue
Moshi Surprise Egg 2012

Shocking Pink
Moshi Surprise Egg 2012

Electric Yellow
Moshi Surprise Egg 2012

Sonic Orange
Moshi Surprise Egg 2012

Wallop

Species: **Jolly Tubthumper**
Set: **Tunies**
Number: **005**
Rarity: **Common**
Variations: **9**

What are they like?
Energetic, rackety and boisterous.

Things to look for:
Thwacktastic body and poised drumsticks.

Classic
Blind Bag/Collectors Pack

Jolly Tubthumpers **love drumming** but have a small problem – the only place they can practise is on their own faces! This, of course, makes these musical Moshlings **quite bonkers.** They love to **walk for miles** whilst banging out marching tunes.

When they're not on tour, Jolly Tubthumpers might be found in Thwackboom Valley where they enjoy **twirling their drumsticks**. They hate being told to "shhh" and they aren't very fond of the blisters their sticks can give them either!

Shocking Pink
Moshi Surprise Egg 2012

Electric Yellow
Moshi Surprise Egg 2012

Where to find 'em:

Ultra Rare
Glitter Green
Blind Bag/Collectors Pack

Glitter Yellow
Blind Bag/Collectors Pack

Brilliant Blue
Moshi Surprise Egg 2012

Special Gold
Blind Bag/Collectors Pack

Sonic Orange
Moshi Surprise Egg 2012

Rox Collection 2
Rox Tin 2013

Blingo

Smooth, happening and **super funky**, Flashy Foxes never take off their shades. But that's not because it's sunny up in Hipsta Hills, it's because the **gleaming bling** they collect is **totally dazzling!**

When these hip little Moshlings are not getting down to the latest cool tracks on their **superfly boom boxes**, they enjoy cruising along Jive Drive and making up silly rhymes in their **lightning-fast street talk...**

Species: **Flashy Fox**
Set: **Secrets**
Number: **103**
Rarity: **Ultra Rare**
Variations: **9**

What are they like?
Offhand, fast-talking and fashion-conscious.

Things to look for:
Baseball hat, boom box, sunglasses and bling.

Where to find 'em:

Ultra Rare

Classic
Blind Bag/Collectors Pack

Ultra Rare

Glitter Green
Blind Bag/Collectors Pack

Glitter Yellow
Blind Bag/Collectors Pack

Rox Collection 1
Rox Tin 2012

Ultra Rare
Red/Yellow Two-Tone Swirl
Super Seeds 2012

Green Two-Tone Swirl
Super Seeds 2012

Ultra Rare

Brilliant Blue
Moshi Surprise Egg 2012

Shocking Pink
Moshi Surprise Egg 2012

Special Gold
Blind Bag/Collectors Pack

Plinky

Species: Squeezy TinkleHuff
Set: Tunies
Number: 106
Rarity: Ultra Rare
Variations: 9
☑

Squeezy TinkleHuffs come from Hurdy Gurdytown but they can often be found **busking in Polka Park.**

These musical Moshlings love to stroll around town, **puffing out merry tunes** and waltzing up and down the streets. But if anyone pushes their buttons, they start to **hiccup out of tune**. They also have a particular dislike of bagpipes.

Things to look for:
Squeezy middle, keyboard head and dancing feet.

What are they like?
Gleeful, harmonious and breathless.

Where to find 'em:

Ultra Rare

Classic
Blind Bag/Collectors Pack

Glitter Green
Blind Bag/Collectors Pack

Glitter Yellow
Blind Bag/Collectors Pack

Ultra Rare

Green Two-Tone Swirl
Super Seeds 2012

Rox Collection 1
Rox Tin 2012

Ultra Rare

Red/Yellow Two-Tone Swirl
Super Seeds 2012

Brilliant Blue
Moshi Surprise Egg 2012

Shocking Pink
Moshi Surprise Egg 2012

Special Gold
Blind Bag/Collectors Pack

Series Two

Wurley

There's nothing a Twirly Tiddlycopter likes more than a cloudless sky. You can see these **tin-skinned flying Moshlings** buzzing about above Monstro City carrying their precious cargoes from A to B. They **love to hum tunes** as they go – especially classical music.

You can sometimes see **swarms of Twirly Tiddlycopters** flying over Nuttanbolt Lake, but they spend most days hovering around Hangar Eight-and-a-Half where they can get their **favourite snack - windsocks dipped in engine oil!**

Species: **Twirly Tiddlycopter**
Set: **Techies**
Number: **105**
Rarity: **Ultra Rare**
Variations: **7**

What are they like?
Daring, noisy and trusting.

Things to look for:
Whirly headgear.

Ultra Rare

Classic
Blind Bag/Collectors Pack

Special Gold
Blind Bag/Collectors Pack

Electric Yellow
Moshi Surprise Egg 2012

Where to find 'em:

Ultra Rare

Glitter Green
Blind Bag/Collectors Pack

Glitter Yellow
Blind Bag/Collectors Pack

Sonic Orange
Moshi Surprise Egg 2012

Rox Collection 1
Rox Tin 2012

111

Roxy

Species: **Precious Prism**
Set: **Secrets**
Number: **101**
Rarity: **Ultra Rare**
Variations: **7**

✓

Where to find 'em:

Things to look for:
Handle-with-care gloves and multi-facets.

Ultra Rare

Classic
Blind Bag/Collectors Pack

What are they like?
Priceless, fastidious and fragile.

Glitter Yellow
Blind Bag/Collectors Pack

Ultra Rare

Glitter Green
Blind Bag/Collectors Pack

✓

Shocking Pink
Moshi Surprise Egg 2012

Sonic Orange
Moshi Surprise Egg 2012

Special Gold
Blind Bag/Collectors Pack

✓

Rox Collection 1
Rox Tin 2012

There's a reason these Moshlings are **ultra-rare** – no one knows where they come from! Some used to think that Precious Prisms came from the **Twinkly-Dink mines** but that was just a rumour.

These **secretive gems** aren't seen that much, as they hide away, afraid of getting smudges on their **beautiful, shiny facets.** They're so scared of this, in fact, that they even wear gloves themselves! But there's a good reason for their fears: they are so fragile they can easily **shatter into sparkly little pieces!**

Series Two

Tingaling

Things to look for:
Magic bell and lucky raised paw.

What are they like?
Generous, auspicious, friendly and wise.

Species: Kitten of Good Fortune
Set: Luckies
Number: 063
Rarity: Rare
Variations: 11 ✓

Where to find 'em:

☐ **Brilliant Blue** Moshi Surprise Egg 2012	☐ **Electric Yellow** Moshi Surprise Egg 2012
☐ **Shocking Pink** Moshi Surprise Egg 2012	☐ **Sonic Orange** Moshi Surprise Egg 2012

Classic
Blind Bag/Collectors Pack

☐ **Christmas Tree Green**
Winter Wonderland

☐ **Special Gold**
Blind Bag/Collectors Pack

Ultra Rare
Glitter Green
Blind Bag/Collectors Pack

Glitter Yellow
Blind Bag/Collectors Pack

✓ **Frostbite Blue**
Winter Wonderland/
Advent Calendar 2012

Kittens of Good Fortune love lying on windowsills and rooftops but if you do find one at ground level, then you are fortunate indeed. **Good luck** will come to anyone who finds a Kitten of Good Fortune, **particularly if its magic neck bell is tinkling.**

These mystic Moshlings spread **delight and joy** wherever they go, with just a wave from one of their paws. Originally from Hong Bong Island, they enjoy reading tea leaves and **feasting on fortune cookies.** The only thing they think of as very bad luck, is meeting Moshling Puppies!

Ultra Rare
Bauble Red
Winter Wonderland

113

Penny

Species: Mini Money
Set: Luckies
Number: 011
Rarity: Common
Variations: 11

If these Moshlings need to make vital decisions, they can be found **flipping themselves high up in the air** deep inside Dime Mine, or sometimes out on Windfall Way. But really these Moshlngs are known for being lucky, whether they land on **heads or tails!**

Luckies love really big pockets and if you find one in yours, **rubbing their tummies** will bring you prosperity! Just don't lose them down the **back of the sofa** or in a slot machine. Mini Monies dislike both of these . . .

What are they like?
Indecisive, ebullient and dizzy.

Things to look for:
Lucky tummy and coin body.

Brilliant Blue
Moshi Surprise Egg 2012

Shocking Pink
Moshi Surprise Egg 2012

Electric Yellow
Moshi Surprise Egg 2012

Sonic Orange
Moshi Surprise Egg 2012

Classic
Blind Bag/Collectors Pack

Christmas Tree Green
Winter Wonderland

Special Gold
Blind Bag/Collectors Pack

Where to find 'em:

Ultra Rare

Glitter Green
Blind Bag/Collectors Pack

Glitter Yellow
Blind Bag/Collectors Pack

Frostbite Blue
Winter Wonderland/
Advent Calendar 2012

Ultra Rare

Bauble Red
Winter Wonderland

Holga

Happy Snappies **love to take photos.** SNAP! They particularly like shooting pictures of the **rich and famous** and using towering tripods to get a steady, perfect image. **FLASH!** And when they're done, they hand out the results for all to see.

Off duty, these **camera-like critters** can be found at 35 Mil Hill, somewhere on Shutter Island, where they unwind with a **relaxing game of lens cap tiddlywinks.** Happy Snappies don't like a lack of focus for long though, and they're soon back to the snapping.

Species: **Happy Snappy**
Set: **Techies**
Number: **045**
Rarity: **Uncommon**
Variations: **11**

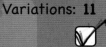

What are they like?
Nosy, quick, bright and friendly.

Things to look for:
Camera body, lens tummy and flashbulb head.

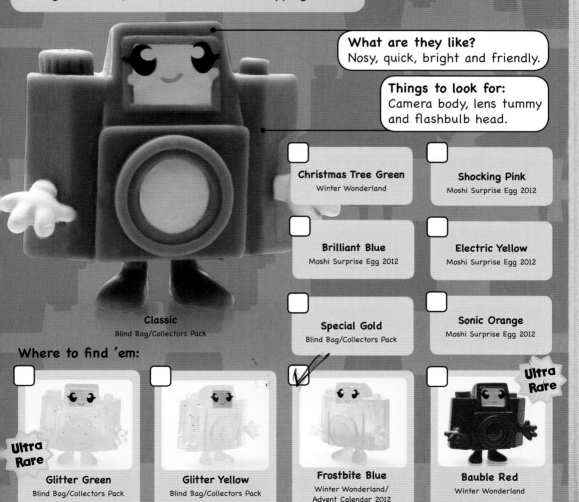

Classic
Blind Bag/Collectors Pack

Christmas Tree Green
Winter Wonderland

Shocking Pink
Moshi Surprise Egg 2012

Brilliant Blue
Moshi Surprise Egg 2012

Electric Yellow
Moshi Surprise Egg 2012

Special Gold
Blind Bag/Collectors Pack

Sonic Orange
Moshi Surprise Egg 2012

Where to find 'em:

Ultra Rare

Glitter Green
Blind Bag/Collectors Pack

Glitter Yellow
Blind Bag/Collectors Pack

Frostbite Blue
Winter Wonderland/
Advent Calendar 2012

Ultra Rare

Bauble Red
Winter Wonderland

115

Pirate Pong

Species: Glump
Number: G04
Variations: 6

What are they like?
Smelly and mischievous.

Pirate Pong is the **smelliest** of all the Glumps. If this **malodourous monstrosity** walks into a crowded room, it'll be clear in a matter of seconds after a **stinky squirt** that reeks of rotten fish!

Things to look for:
Spiky hair and pirate eye patch.

Where to find 'em:

Special Gold
Blind Bag/Collectors Pack

Classic
Blind Bag/Collectors Pack

Glitter Yellow
Blind Bag/Collectors Pack

Ultra Rare

Glitter Green
Blind Bag/Collectors Pack

Shocking Pink
Moshi Surprise Egg 2012

Electric Yellow
Moshi Surprise Egg 2012

Series Two

Bloopy

Species: Glump
Number: G05
Variations: 6

Things to look for:
Tufty hair and freckles.

What are they like?
Ferocious, sad and bad!

Classic
Blind Bag/Collectors Pack

Where to find 'em:

Bloopy likes nothing better than **splatting Moshlings** with Mega Glump Thumps. Perhaps it's because this badly behaved blob feels blue. But so would you if you had a face like a **squished blueberry!**

Special Gold
Blind Bag/Collectors Pack

Glitter Yellow
Blind Bag/Collectors Pack

Ultra Rare

Glitter Green
Blind Bag/Collectors Pack

Shocking Pink
Moshi Surprise Egg 2012

Electric Yellow
Moshi Surprise Egg 2012

Fabio

Species: **Glump**
Number: **G07**
Variations: **6**

☑

Apart from perfecting that **ridiculous pink quiff** and eating, this mindless Glump is also capable of crunching enemies in seconds with a **Triple Tooth TerrorBite.** Foolish Fabio has even tried eating his own teeth but they tasted, well, toothy!

What are they like?
Goofy and silly.

Things to look for:
Three big teeth and a single tuft of hair.

Where to find 'em:

Classic
Blind Bag/Collectors Pack

Special Gold
Blind Bag/Collectors Pack

Ultra Rare

Glitter Yellow
Blind Bag/Collectors Pack

Glitter Green
Blind Bag/Collectors Pack

Shocking Pink
Moshi Surprise Egg 2012

Electric Yellow
Moshi Surprise Egg 2012

Fishlips

Species: **Glump**
Number: G02
Variations: **6**

Things to look for:
Sad frown and only one eye.

What are they like?
Floppy, sad and lonely!

Classic
Blind Bag/Collectors Pack

Special Gold
Blind Bag/Collectors Pack

Where to find 'em:

Glitter Yellow
Blind Bag/Collectors Pack

Ultra Rare

Glitter Green
Blind Bag/Collectors Pack

Shocking Pink
Moshi Surprise Egg 2012

Electric Yellow
Moshi Surprise Egg 2012

Cheer up Fishlips! Or is it **difficult to smile** with those juicy jaws? This cyclops' chops are perpetually sealed with **gunk and gloop** – perfect for delivering a slimy smacker. **Yuck!**

Podge

Species: Glump
Number: G06
Variations: 9

Things to look for:
Sad eyes and an unhappy pout.

What are they like?
A little glum and oh so cute.

With Podge around, there's danger of ending up in a **tangle of tacky tongue.** This bouncing Glump has a super-long lasso in his mouth and he **knows how to use it!**

Classic
Blind Bag/Collectors Pack

Where to find 'em:

Ultra Rare

Glitter Green
Blind Bag/Collectors Pack

Glitter Yellow
Blind Bag/Collectors Pack

Special Gold
Blind Bag/Collectors Pack/
Covermount - Issue 22 of *Moshi Monsters Magazine*

Christmas Tree Green
Winter Wonderland

Electric Yellow
Moshi Surprise Egg 2012

Brilliant Blue
Moshi Surprise Egg 2012

Frostbite Blue
Winter Wonderland/
Advent Calendar 2012

Ultra Rare

Bauble Red
Winter Wonderland

Rocko

Talk about a **Grumpy Glump!** There's no pleasing some Glumps, particularly this one. This **boinging brute** hangs out on his own or attacks others with a Rocko Blocko Backroll because he just **hates everything.**

Species: **Glump**
Number: **G01**
Variations: **9**

What are they like?
Feisty, grumpy and fond of jazz music.

Where to find 'em:

Ultra Rare
Glitter Green
Blind Bag/Collectors Pack

Glitter Yellow
Blind Bag/Collectors Pack

Special Gold
Blind Bag/Collectors Pack/ Covermount - Issue 22 of *Moshi Monsters Magazine*

Christmas Tree Green
Winter Wonderland

Classic
Blind Bag/Collectors Pack

Things to look for:
A big scar and one lower fang.

Electric Yellow
Moshi Surprise Egg 2012

Brilliant Blue
Moshi Surprise Egg 2012

Frostbite Blue
Winter Wonderland/ Advent Calendar 2012

Ultra Rare
Bauble Red
Winter Wonderland

121

Squiff

Species: Glump
Number: G03
Variations: 8

What are they like?
Smelly and awkward.

Things to look for:
Three bulbous eyes and two buck teeth.

Three eyes, buck teeth and an ill-advised hairdo – it must be Squiff! This **wayward weirdo** tries to be friendly, but no one wants to hang around when Squiff lets rip with a **Squiffy Stinkbomb!** Eeew!

Classic
Blind Bag/Collectors Pack

Where to find 'em:

Ultra Rare

Glitter Green
Blind Bag/Collectors Pack

Glitter Yellow
Blind Bag/Collectors Pack

Special Gold
Blind Bag/Collectors Pack/
Covermount – Issue 22 of *Moshi Monsters Magazine*

Electric Yellow
Moshi Surprise Egg 2012

Brilliant Blue
Moshi Surprise Egg 2012

Frostbite Blue
Winter Wonderland/
Advent Calendar 2012

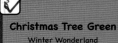

Christmas Tree Green
Winter Wonderland

Bauble Red
Winter Wonderland

Ultra Rare

Mustachio

Species: Glump
Number: G08
Variations: 9

What are they like?
Moustached, bullying and bossy boots.

Is that facial fuzz for real or is it just a **terrible disguise?** Who knows, because Mustachio is too busy barking orders and attacking Moshlings with **scritchy-scratchy Bristly Brush Offs** to answer silly questions.

Things to look for:
A massive moustache and a chunky monobrow.

Classic
Blind Bag/Collectors Pack

Where to find 'em:

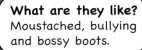

Ultra Rare

Glitter Green
Blind Bag/Collectors Pack

Glitter Yellow
Blind Bag/Collectors Pack

Special Gold
Blind Bag/Collectors Pack/
Covermount - Issue 22 of Moshi
Monsters Magazine

Christmas Tree Green
Winter Wonderland

Ultra Rare

Electric Yellow
Moshi Surprise Egg 2012

Brilliant Blue
Moshi Surprise Egg 2012

Frostbite Blue
Winter Wonderland/
Advent Calendar 2012

Bauble Red
Winter Wonderland

123

Freak Face

Species: **Glump**
Number: **G12**
Variations: **6**

When it comes to dribbling, no Glump is better than Freak Face. He likes to **drench his enemies** in the most dire drool and then run away laughing his **evil laugh.**

What are they like?
A dribbling mess.

Things to look for:
Dribble, dribble and more dribble.

Classic
Blind Bag/Collectors Pack

Special Gold
Blind Bag/Collectors Pack

Where to find 'em:

Glitter Yellow
Blind Bag/Collectors Pack

Ultra Rare

Glitter Green
Blind Bag/Collectors Pack

Brilliant Blue
Moshi Surprise Egg 2012

✓

Electric Yellow
Moshi Surprise Egg 2012

Black Jack

Species: Glump
Number: G11
Variations: 6

What are they like?
Very mean, evil tempered and calculated.

Things to look for:
Big set of gnashers and scary red eyes.

Classic
Blind bag/collectors pack

Where to find 'em:

Black Jack is known as the **meanest Glump** in Monstro City. Even the other Glumps fear his fearsome **Cannonball Cavalcade attack!**

Special Gold
Blind Bag/Collectors Pack

Glitter Yellow
Blind Bag/Collector's Pack

Ultra Rare

Glitter Green
Blind Bag/Collectors Pack

Brilliant Blue
Moshi Surprise Egg 2012

Electric Yellow
Moshi Surprise Egg 2012

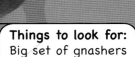

125

Ned

Species: **Glump**
Number: **G10**
Variations: **6**

Things to look for:
Flying goggles and a blinging gold tooth.

What are they like?
Not as geeky as you would think.

Classic
Blind Bag/Collectors Pack

Where to find 'em:

At first sight, Ned looks like he might be a **bit of a nerd!** But don't be fooled. He might wear **daft goggles** but this Glump can still give you a run for your money. (You'll be running away, mostly.)

☐ **Special Gold**
Blind Bag/Collectors Pack

☐ **Glitter Yellow**
Blind Bag/Collectors Pack

Ultra Rare

☐ **Glitter Green**
Blind Bag/Collectors Pack

☐ **Brilliant Blue**
Moshi Surprise Egg 2012

☐ **Electric Yellow**
Moshi Surprise Egg 2012

Series Two

Bruiser

Bruiser likes nothing more than to cause mayhem with his **Scarface Smashes** and **Scowling ScrimScrams.** He's also one of the most **untidy** Glumps. But then, being evil can take up a lot of time . . .

Species: **Glump**
Number: **G00**
Variations: **6**

What are they like?
Messy, untidy and always running late.

Classic
Blind Bag/Collectors Pack

Things to look for:
Criss-crossed plaster and a frown.

Special Gold
Blind Bag/Collectors Pack

Where to find 'em:

Glitter Yellow
Blind Bag/Collectors Pack

Ultra Rare

Glitter Green
Blind Bag/Collectors Pack

Brilliant Blue
Moshi Surprise Egg 2012

Electric Yellow
Moshi Surprise Egg 2012

Ratty

Set: **Additional Characters**
Number: **M15**
Variations: **4**

Wherever you find Ratty, you'll also find Bug. And wherever you find Ratty and Bug, **mayhem can't be far behind.** They love to cause mischief: stealing Pepperbombs from The Pepperbomb Geyser to make everyone sneeze or sneaking into the Unnatural History Museum and **re-arranging the dinosaur bones** to form new creatures! **You have been warned . . .**

What is he like?
Loyal, chaotic and sneaky.

Things to look for:
Big ears, big teeth and three blue eyes.

Where to find 'em:

Special Gold
Blind Bag/Collectors Pack

Shocking Pink
Moshi Surprise Egg 2012

Brilliant Blue
Moshi Surprise Egg 2012

Classic
Blind Bag/Collectors Pack

Bug

What is he like?
Silly, naughty and irritating.

Set: **Additional Characters**
Number: **M14**
Variations: **4**

Things to look for:
Bug-eyes, rubbery lips and exoskeletal spikes.

Classic
Blind Bag/Collectors Pack

Where to find 'em:

Special Gold
Blind Bag/Collectors Pack

Sonic Orange
Moshi Surprise Egg 2012

Electric Yellow
Moshi Surprise Egg 2012

Bug is Ratty's **partner in crime.** They are almost inseparable and always up to mischief – although never as naughty as any Glump or C.L.O.N.C. agent. Bug is a prankster and **loves practical jokes.**

If he's not causing chaos in one of Monstro Cities public places, he's usually **stocking up on stink bombs** and itching powder.

Art Lee

Set: Additional Character
Number: **M16**
Variations: **4**

Things to look for:
Spray cans, gloopy paint and mess everywhere.

What is he like?
Artistic, underground and sneaky.

Classic
Blind Bag/Collectors Pack

Where to find 'em:

Special Gold
Blind Bag/Collectors Pack

Sonic Orange
Moshi Surprise Egg 2012

Electric Yellow
Moshi Surprise Egg 2012

Art Lee is an amateur graffiti artist, working towards being **Monstro City's next Danksy.** Art spends his time in the Underground Caves, creating super-sweet works of pop art and is well known for being able to eat **Spider Lollies in one bite!**

130

Roland Jones

Set: **Additional Character**
Number: **M20**
Variations: **4**

What is he like?
Bubbly, windy and funny.

Things to look for:
Rattling bottles, hiccups and burps.

Classic
Blind Bag Collectors Pack

Roland Jones is **obsessed with Wobble Ade!** He is convinced it will cause growth spurts and is jealous of his siblings who are more than twice his size. He buys a new bottle of Wobble Ade every fifteen minutes. With all that **sloshy pop** in his belly, he's often seen (and heard) rolling home.

Where to find 'em:

Special Gold
Blind Bag Collectors Pack

Brilliant Blue
Moshi Surprise Egg 2012

Shocking Pink
Moshi Surprise Egg 2012

Gabby

Species: **Mini Moshifone**
Set: **Techies**
Number: **025**
Rarity: **Common**
Variations: **6**

In the depths of the mysterious Voltage Vaults, where the **atmosphere is electric,** you'll find Mini Moshifones recharging their batteries. Loaded with cool apps, these **chatty cell phones** are always nattering to their buddies and sending funny texts. LOL!

Mini Moshifones also love to **compose fancy new ringtones** but there's nothing they like better than making calls and **helping monsters connect** with one another.

Things to look for:
Push buttons, awesome apps and shiny screen.

What are they like?
Chatty, tech-savvy and obliging.

Classic
Blind Bag Collectors Pack

Ultra
Rare

Platinum Exclusive Edition
Official Collectable Figures Guide

Series Three

Where to find 'em:

Special Gold
Blind Bag/Collectors Pack

Shocking Pink
Moshi Surprise Egg 2012

Brilliant Blue
Moshi Surprise Egg 2012

Rox UK
Rox Collector Tin 2

133

Shrewman

Set: **Additional Characters**
Number: **M18**
Variations: **4**

Things to look for:
Shaggy hair with lots of curls.

What is he like?
Shy, helpful, and very clever.

Classic
Blind Bag/Collectors Pack

Where to find 'em:

Special Gold
Blind Bag/Collectors Pack

Brilliant Blue
Moshi Surprise Egg 2012

Shocking Pink
Moshi Surprise Egg 2012

If you go down to the woods today you might just spot the Shrewman. Shy but helpful, this **berry-loving critter** rarely leaves the comfort of his tree trunk home - and nor would you if you were **busy writing books** on your tippy-tappy typewriter. In fact, some say the Shrewman uses berry juice as ink because he's **too scared to go to the shops.**

Series Three

Agony Ant

A gaggle of Woolly Blue Hoodoos and a few Furry Heebees taught Agony Ant everything they know about **fortune-telling** up in Hokery Pokery Heights. Now she graces the pages of *The Daily Growl* regularly to **bestow her wisdom** onto its readers.

Set: Additional Character
Number: M17
Variations: 4

Things to look for:
Anty antennae and big glasses.

Where to find 'em:

Special Gold
Blind Bag/Collectors Pack

Sonic Orange
Moshi Surprise Egg 2012

Electric Yellow
Moshi Surprise Egg 2012

What is she like?
Wise, upbeat and friendly.

Classic
Blind Bag/Collectors Pack

135

Nipper

Species: Titchy TrundleBot
Set: Techies
Number: 108
Rarity: Ultra Rare
Variations: 4

As well as helping to build Monstro City, Titchy TrundleBots can **pluck Rox from the highest trees,** trundle across bumpy surfaces and warn Monsters of falling boulders.

Their fully manoeuvrable arms, caterpillar track shoes and flashing lights make them **right at home on construction sites.** But the place the Titchy TrundleBots call home is Quivering Quarry where they **chase each other around playing tag all day!**

Things to look for:
Safety-first flashing lights, grabbing hands, tracked feet and a big heart!

What are they like?
Grabby, zippy, versatile and hard-working.

Ultra
Rare

Where to find 'em:

Classic
Blind Bag/Collectors Pack

Special Gold
Blind Bag/Collectors Pack

Sonic Orange
Moshi Surprise Egg 2012

Electric Yellow
Moshi Surprise Egg 2012

Colonel Catcher

Things to look for:
Massive moustache, monocle and safari hat.

Set: **Additional Characters**
Number: **M13**
Variations: **4**

What is he like?
Obsessed with Flutterbies.

Classic
Blind Bag/Collectors Pack

Where to find 'em:

Special Gold
Blind Bag/Collectors Pack

Sonic Orange
Moshi Surprise Egg 2012

Electric Yellow
Moshi Surprise Egg 2012

Obsessed with pinning Flutterby species to his Genus of Monstro City whiteboard, Colonel Catcher **retired early from Bendia**, and can be found roaming Flutterby Field with shouts of exasperation as he **tries to catch new beauties.**

Lenny Lard

Set: Additional Characters
Number: M22
Variations: 4

What is he like?
Boastful and big-headed.

Things to look for:
His rubber ring.

Challenged by his schoolmates to become **Monstro City's first youth diver,** Lenny Lard has been practising in the waters of The Port ever since. Even though he can't yet swim it's said he can **project himself out of the water like a rocket ship.** Though only when you're not watching.

Classic
Blind Bag/Collectors Pack

Where to find 'em:

Special Gold
Blind Bag/Collectors Pack

Sonic Orange
Moshi Surprise Egg 2012

Electric Yellow
Moshi Surprise Egg 2012

Myrtle

Species: **Diving Turtle**
Set: **Additional Characters**
Number: **M21**
Variations: **4**

Myrtle the Diving Turtle is world-renowned for her **treasure hunting ability.** Her great finds have included one teapot, a shoelace and a pool table where she **plays weekly matches** with her mates.

Things to look for:
Diving mask and green shell.

What is she like?
Relentless, curious and breath-taking!

Where to find 'em:

Special Gold
Blind Bag/Collectors Pack

Sonic Orange
Moshi Surprise Egg 2012

Electric Yellow
Moshi Surprise Egg 2012

Classic
Blind Bag/Collectors Pack

Clutch

Set: **Additional Characters**
Number: **M19**
Variations: **4**

☑

Clutch has been **delivering gifts** from Gift Island for almost thirty years. Well past the point of retiring, his **love for smiling Monster Owners** keeps him coming back day after day.

Where to find 'em:

☑

Special Gold
Blind Bag/Collectors Pack

☐

Brilliant Blue
Moshi Surprise Egg 2012

☐

Shocking Pink
Moshi Surprise Egg 2012

What is he like?
Punctual and surprisingly strong.

Things to look for:
White cap and heavy sack bursting with gifts from Gift Island.

Classic
Blind Bag/Collectors Pack

ClueKoo

Species: **Cluekoo**
Set: **Additional Characters**
Number: **M12**
Variations: 4

Things to look for:
Top-notch topknot, tiny wings and itty-bitty beak.

What are they like?
Green-fingered, generous and gifted.

Where to find 'em:

Special Gold
Blind Bag/Collectors Pack

Classic
Blind Bag/Collectors Pack

Sonic Orange
Moshi Surprise Egg 2012

Electric Yellow
Moshi Surprise Egg 2012

Even green-thumbed Monsters **need a little help sometimes,** so thankfully there's the Cluekoo who lives in your Moshling Garden. The Cluekoo watches everything that goes on when you're not there and will tell you if any little Moshlings have **been by for a nibble.**

141

Herman Crab

Things to look for:
Hard shell and beautiful blue eyes.

Set: **Additional Characters**
Number: **M11**
Variations: **4**

What is he like?
Shy and retiring, except with crab friends.

Where to find 'em:

Special Gold
Blind Bag/Collectors Pack

Sonic Orange
Moshi Surprise Egg 2012

Electric Yellow
Moshi Surprise Egg 2012

Classic
Blind Bag/Collectors Pack

This **crabby little fella** can usually be found hanging out in the sun on Bleurgh Beach or **paddling in its rock pools** with his friends.

Tomba

Wintery, wistful Snowtots are usually found chilling out on Mount Sillimanjaro, but when they get **fed up with the funny bunnies nibbling their noses** they sometimes migrate to the Frostipop Glacier (to go curling).

You may not be surprised to learn that these moping Moshlings are not fond of central heating, but **singing sad songs** sometimes helps cool them back down.

Species: Wistful Snowtot
Set: Snowies
Number: 073
Rarity: Rare
Variations: 2

What are they like?
Frosty, nervous and melancholy.

Things to look for:
Carrot nose, beanie hat, glove hands and coal eyes.

Where to find 'em: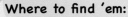

Classic
Blind Bag/Collectors Pack

Special Gold
Blind Bag/Collectors Pack

143

Leo

Species: **Abominable Snowling**
Set: **Snowies**
Number: **098**
Rarity: **Ultra Rare**
Variations: **2**

Ultra Rare

What are they like?
Perky, misunderstood and lonely.

Classic
Blind Bag/Collectors Pack

Things to look for:
Colourful bobble hats and super soft fur.

Where to find 'em:

Special Gold
Blind Bag/Collectors Pack

Not so much abominable as **really rather friendly,** Abominable Snowlings love snowy games of all kinds. They can usually be found on Mount Sillimanjaro **making ice sculptures** or snowmen, **decorating their igloos** with chocolate sprinkles or chucking snowballs.

What colour are they really? Nobody knows, because Titchy-Tusked Mammoths spend most evenings **dyeing their fur with inka inka essence** and dipping their ears and feet in **gloopy green puddles.** They can even unscrew their tusks and **remove their woolly blue coats** if they get too warm.

Woolly

Species: **Titchy-Tusked Mammoth**
Set: **Snowies**
Number: **058**
Rarity: **Rare**
Variations: **2**

What are they like?
Fluffy, snuffly and timid.

Things to look for:
Titchy tusks and trails of inka inka essence.

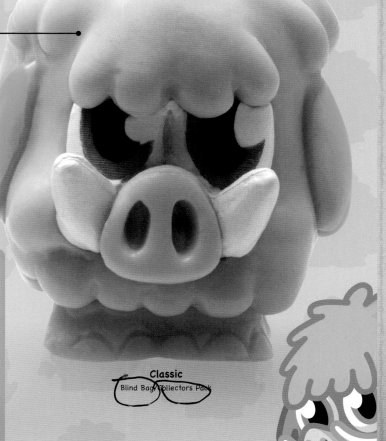

Where to find 'em:

Special Gold
Blind Bag/Collectors Pack

Classic
Blind Bag/Collectors Pack

145

Zack Binspin

Species: **Moptop Tweenybop**
Number: **107**
Rarity: **Ultra Rare**
Variations: **2**

What is he like?
Musical, young and gifted.

Things to look for:
Moptop hair and tweenybopper threads.

ZACK

Classic
Blind Bag/Collectors Pack

Where to find 'em:

Special Gold
Blind Bag/Collectors Pack

Zack has **dreamt of being a famous singer** ever since he saw Screech McPiehole yelling on *Top of the Mops*. And now, thanks to his **high-trousered mentor** Simon Growl, that dream is finally a reality.

Zack **used to sing backing vocals** for one of Monstro City's biggest bin-bound singers, but **solo gooperstardom** beckoned the second he was signed by HighPants Productions. Zack comes from Brashcan Alley but hangs out at the Sandy Drain Hotel these days.

Series Four

Bobbi SingSong

With his smash hit 'Welcome to Jollywood' which, incidentally, is **jolly good,** Bobbi SingSong has found fame. With Jollywood having adopted his number one as their **national anthem,** he has become a **living legend** in his homeland. When he's not meditating, he mostly **whoops it up with his sitar.** Just don't offer him a glass of Wobble-ade or suggest any dilly-dallying!

Species: **Jollywood Singaling**
Number: **112**
Rarity: **Ultra Rare**
Variations: **2**

What is he like?
Jolly, doolally and serene.

Things to look for:
Dazzling hair, disco suit and dancing shoes.

Ultra Rare

Where to find 'em:

Special Gold
Blind Bag/Collectors Pack

Classic
Blind Bag/Collectors Pack

O'Really

Species: Unlucky Larrikin
Set: Luckies
Number: 070
Rarity: Rare
Variations: 2

Things to look for:
Top hat, unlucky shamrock, bristling beard and woeful walking stick.

Where to find 'em:

Special Gold
Blind Bag/Collectors Pack

Classic
Blind Bag/Collectors Pack

What are they like?
Lucky, optimistic and whimsical.

If you see an Unlucky Larrikin coming towards you - go the other way! Their constant whistling, limerick reciting and **joke telling may be uplifting** (briefly) but if you're feeling lucky, it won't have anything to do with these rainbow-hugging critters. They **aren't keen on gold paint** and breakfast cereal, but they are usually cheerful about everything else – even if they are the **most unfortunate Moshlings** of them all! To avoid your own misfortune, you may want to stay away from the fabled Barmy Stone of Shamrock Bog where the Unlucky Larrikins' **soporific story-telling skills** may bore you to tears.

Scrumpy

When they're not nosing around Monstro City, **solving mysteries** and investigating strange goings-on, Surreal Snoopers really can be found **doing the strangest things.** From riding pasta unicycles, to wearing shoes on their heads, they're **surreal by nature** and not just by name!

Species: **Surreal Snooper**
Set: **Arties**
Number: **041**
Rarity: **Uncommon**
Variations: **2**

What are they like?
Investigative, nosy and surreal.

Things to look for:
Bowler hat and super-smart moustache.

Where to find 'em:

Classic
Blind Bag/Collectors Pack

Special Gold
Blind Bag/Collectors Pack

Suey

Species: **Bashful Bowlhead**
Set: **Munchies**
Number: **110**
Rarity: **Ultra Rare**
Variations: **2**

☑

What are they like?
Slurpy, spicy and flavourful.

Things to look for:
Chopsticks and
overflowing noodles.

Ultra
Rare

Classic
Blind Bag/Collectors Pack

Where to find 'em:

Special Gold
Blind Bag/Collectors Pack

These shy but popular Moshlings are **handy to have around,** especially when your **tummy is grumbling,** as they produce a never-ending supply of **slurp-tastic noodles** from their heads! Keep an eye out for them in Won Ton Bay on Hong Bong Island.

CocoLoco

Species: **Naughty Nutter**
Set: **Nutties**
Number: **109**
Rarity: **Ultra Rare**
Variations: **2**

Ultra Rare

What are they like?
Nutty, noisy and fun.

Things to look for:
Bendy straw and nutty stare.

Classic
Blind Bag/Collectors Pack

Where to find 'em:

Special Gold
Blind Bag/Collectors Pack

These nutty little Moshlings **love to party!** Sipping bongo-colada from their heads all day makes them **slightly nuts** and prone to dancing the conga, organizing limbo competitions and shaking their home-made maracas!

151

Pocito

Species: Mini Mangler
Set: Sporties
Number: 111
Rarity: Ultra Rare
Variations: 2

☑

Ultra Rare

Things to look for:
Lycra jumpsuit and mask.

What are they like?
Athletic, strong and rubbery.

Classic
Blind Bag/Collectors Pack

Where to find 'em:

Special Gold
Blind Bag/Collectors Pack

These **mysterious masked Moshlings** just can't stop wrestling! They train at a secret training camp near the giant haystacks of El Astico Ranch, but **don't disturb their fun** or you might find yourself in a spinning headlock or a short-arm scissorlock.

Shelly

Species: **Nattering Nutling**
Set: **Nutties**
Number: **012**
Rarity: **Common**
Variations: **2**

Things to look for:
Fluttering eyelashes and pretty bow.

What are they like?
Gossipy and excitable.

Classic
Blind Bag/Collectors Pack

Where to find 'em:

Special Gold
Blind Bag/Collectors Pack

Nattering Nutlings are **nuts about Moshi celebrities** like Zack Binspin and Bobbi SingSong, and are always desperate to collect autographs of their favourite stars. They love reading *The Daily Growl* and *Shrillboard Magazine* to **keep up with all the latest gossip.**

Judder

Species: **Unhinged Jackhammer**
Set: **Noises**
Number: **014**
Rarity: **Common**
Variations: **2**

What are they like?
Noisy, shuddering and irritating.

Where to find 'em:

Special Gold
Blind Bag/Collectors Pack

Things to look for:
Hard hat and manic grin.

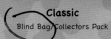

Classic
Blind Bag/Collectors Pack

These manic Moshlings **love boinging up and down** in the road and smashing up the streets. Handle with care, as they're **hard to control** even for the most skilled Roarkers.

These happy, huggy hairballs are **lovin'**
the huggin'! In fact, they'll hug anything
– trees, buildings, random people minding
their own business – frankly my dears,
they're **really not fussy!**

Scarlet O'Haira

Species: **Fluffy Snuggler**
Set: **Mythies**
Number: **067**
Rarity: **Rare**
Variations: **2**

Things to look for:
Fluff and big blue eyes.

Classic
Blind Bag/Collectors Pack

What are they like?
Snuggly, cuddly and fluffy.

Where to find 'em:

Special Gold
Blind Bag/Collectors Pack

Fizzy

Species: **Lipsmacking Bubbly**
Set: **Munchies**
Number: **076**
Rarity: **Rare**
Variations: **2**

Things to look for:
Bubbles and bendy straw.

What are they like?
Sparkling, tasty and unpredictable.

These madcap Moshlings are **fizzy beyond belief!** The bendy straw sticking out of their lids isn't just for **drinking their bubbly goodness** though, it also allows some of the gas to escape so they don't blow their tops!

Where to find 'em:

Special Gold
Blind Bag/Collectors Pack

Classic
Blind Bag/Collectors Pack

Oompah

These **melodious Moshlings** love tooting tunes, **burping rainbow-coloured bubbles** and generally parping around Polka Park and Windypop Place.

Species: **Brassy Blowy Thing**
Set: **Tunies**
Number: **069**
Rarity: **Rare**
Variations: **2**

Where to find 'em:

Special Gold
Blind Bag/Collectors Pack

Things to look for:
Mouthpiece.

Classic
Blind Bag/Collectors Pack

What are they like?
Musical, parping and boisterous.

Betty

Species: **Yodelling MooMoo**
Set: **Noises**
Number: **037**
Rarity: **Uncommon**
Variations: **2**

☑

Things to look for:
Horns and a big mouth!

What are they like?
Loud and diva-ish.

Classic
Blind Bag/Collectors Pack

Where to find 'em:

Special Gold
Blind Bag/Collectors Pack

Yodelling MooMoos can be heard from miles around, thanks to their **ear-splitting yodels.** All that noise can be dangerous though, as they tend to live on snowy mountains and the **racket can cause avalanches!**

Boomer

Species: Bigmouth Squiddly Dee
Set: Noises
Number: 035
Rarity: Uncommon
Variations: 2

Things to look for:
Toilet roll bandages.

What are they like?
Sensitive and slightly deaf.

Classic
Blind Bag/Collectors Pack

Where to find 'em:

Special Gold
Blind Bag/Collectors Pack

Bigmouth Squiddly Dees are **SERIOUSLY loud** and even wear bandages over their own ears to protect themselves from the amount of noise they make. Their **blaring shrieks** have made them a little hard of hearing, so **speak up** if you want to be heard!

159

Shambles

What are they like?
Shambolic and slightly mad.

Species: **Scrappy Chappy**
Set: **Mythies**
Number: **016**
Rarity: **Common**
Variations: **2**

Things to look for:
Nibbled ears and mismatched eyes.

Classic
Blind Bag/Collectors Pack

Where to find 'em:

Special Gold
Blind Bag/Collectors Pack

These **shambolic furballs** look like they've been dragged through a hedge backwards, forwards, sideways and upside down. Which is not far from the truth, as their **favourite sport is hedge diving!**

Series Four

160

Rooby

These **paw-swinging Moshlings** will do almost anything to protect the soft toys stuffed with jellybeans that they keep in their pouches. With their **lightning-fast fists and fancy footwork,** Plucky PunchaRoos love a scrap!

Species: **Plucky PunchaRoo**
Set: **Sporties**
Number: **062**
Rarity: **Rare**
Variations: **2**

Where to find 'em:

Special Gold
Blind Bag/Collectors Pack

Things to look for:
Boxing gloves and titchy purple critter.

Classic
Blind Bag/Collectors Pack

What are they like?
Bouncy and protective.

HipHop

Species: **Blaring Boombox**
Set: **Tunies**
Number: **036**
Rarity: **Uncommon**
Variations: **2**

What are they like?
Funky, old-school and rockin'.

Things to look for:
Speakers, buttons and aerial.

Classic
Blind Bag/Collectors Pack

Where to find 'em:

Special Gold
Blind Bag/Collectors Pack

These playful noisemakers **boogie all day and all night** to the music blaring out from their speakers. Blaring Boomboxes **love to share their music** with other Moshlings, whether they're interested in it or not!

Busling

You can try **putting an arm out to stop them** but you can't actually get on a Bustling Busling because they're too small! These mechanical Moshlings are at their happiest bustling around on a clear road, eating **diesel-filled doughnuts** and getting annoyed by bicycles. The best place to see them is on Main Street, where you will have to hang around for ages but then **three usually turn up at once.**

Species: **Bustling Busling**
Number: **004**
Rarity: **Common**
Variations: 2

Things to look for:
The wheels on the bus going round and round.

What are they like?
Titchy and stressed.

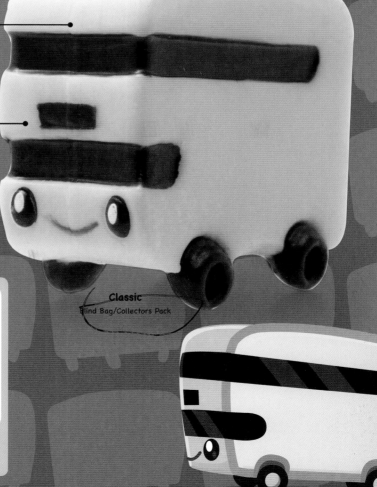

Classic
Blind Bag/Collectors Pack

Where to find 'em:

Special Gold
Blind Bag/Collectors Pack

Rofl

Species: **Jabbering Jibberling**
Set: **Smilies**
Number: **029**
Rarity: **Uncommon**
Variations: **2**

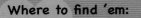

They love a corn on the cob and a **good tongue-twister** and boy can these Jabbering Jibberlings talk! All mouth and teeth, these Moshlings can produce the most **glorious amount of gabbling gibberish.**

Short of pulling a woolly hat firmly over your ears, there's not a lot you can do to **curb the continuous chattering.** They hate dental floss and slow-dancing, so you could always try one of those?

Where to find 'em:

Special Gold
Blind Bag/Collectors Pack

Things to look for:
Chattering teeth!

What are they like?
Gabby, gobby and gibbering.

Classic
Blind Bag/Collectors Pack

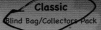

Congratulations!

You've reached the end of **The Official Collectable Figures Guide**, but have you reached the end of your collection? Only the top Moshling collectors like Monstro City's finest, **Buster Bumblechops**, are capable of tracking down every single character! (We've heard he keeps them lined up on shelves in the bathroom at his ranch so he can play with them in the bath!)

Use the following pages to keep an **at-a-glance record** of your collection and spot the **gaps you need to fill**. Maybe that elusive character could be in the next Blind Bag you pick up, or perhaps you could swap some at school. They're all out there somewhere, you've just got to **keep looking!**

There are sure to be more figures to come so **the fun isn't over yet**. Long may the collecting continue!

Good luck!

Series One - At a Glance

Classic/Ultimate Collection/Zoo 2012												
Glitter Purple												
Glitter Orange												
Special Gold												
Glow-in-the-Dark Scream Green												
Glow-in-the-Dark Voodoo Blue												
Glow-in-the-Dark Ghost White												
Special Pumpkin Heads												
Green Two-Tone Swirl												
Red/Yellow Two-Tone Swirl												
Frostbite Blue												
Bauble Red												
Limited Edition Goshi Moshi Blue												
Goo Green												
Twistmas Edition												
Brilliant Blue												
Shocking Pink												
Sonic Orange												
Electric Yellow												
Rox Collection												
Christmas Tree Green												
Glitter Red Moshi Magazine Exclusive												

	1	2	3	4	5	6	7	8	9	10	11	12
Classic/Ultimate Collection/Zoo 2012	☑	☑	☐	☑	☑	☑	☑	☑	☑	☑	☐	☑
Glitter Purple	☐	☐	☐	☐	☐	☐	☐	☐	☐	☐	☐	☐
Glitter Orange	☐	☐	☐	☐	☐	☐	☐	☐	☐	☐	☐	☐
Special Gold	☐	☐	☐	☐	☐	☐	☐	☐	☐	☐	☐	☐
Glow-in-the-Dark Scream Green	☐	☐	☐	☐	☐	☐	☐	☐	☐	☑	☐	☐
Glow-in-the-Dark Voodoo Blue	☐	☑	☐	☐	☐	☐	☐	☐	☐	☐	☐	☐
Glow-in-the-Dark Ghost White	☐	☐	☐	☐	☐	☐	☐	☐	☐	☐	☐	☐
Special Pumpkin Heads	☐	☐	☐	☐	☐	☐	☐	☐	☐	☐	☐	☐
Green Two-Tone Swirl				☐	☐	☐	☐	☐	☐	☐	☐	
Red/Yellow Two-Tone Swirl				☐	☐	☐	☐	☐	☐		☐	
Frostbite Blue												☐
Bauble Red												☐
Limited Edition Goshi Moshi Blue									☐			
Goo Green									☐			
Twistmas Edition							☑					
Brilliant Blue				☐	☐	☐	☐	☐	☐		☐	☐
Shocking Pink	☐	☐	☐	☐	☐	☐	☐	☐	☐	☐	☑	☐
Sonic Orange	☐	☐	☐									☐
Electric Yellow												☐
Rox Collection	☑										☐	
Christmas Tree Green												☐
Glitter Red Moshi Magazine Exclusive												

167

Series One – At a Glance

	1	2	3	4	5	6	7	8	9	10	11	12
Classic/Ultimate Collection/Zoo 2012	▨	▨	▨	▨	▨	▨	▨	▨	▨	▨	▨	▨
Glitter Purple	☐	☐	☐	☐	☐	☐	☐	☐	☐	☐	☐	☐
Glitter Orange	☐	☐	☐	☐	☐	☐	☐	☐	☐	☐	☐	☐
Special Gold	☐	☐	☐	▨	☐	☐	☐	☐	☐	☐	☐	☐
Glow-in-the-Dark Scream Green	☐	☐	☐	☐	☐	☐	☐	☐	☐	☐	☐	☐
Glow-in-the-Dark Voodoo Blue	☐	☐	☐	☐	☐	☐	☐	☐	☐	☐	☐	☐
Glow-in-the-Dark Ghost White	▨	☐	☐	☐	☐	☐	☐	☐	☐	☐	☐	☐
Special Pumpkin Heads	☐	☐	☐	☐	☐	☐	☐	☐	☐	☐	☐	☐
Green Two-Tone Swirl								☐	☐	☐	☐	☐
Red/Yellow Two-Tone Swirl								☐	☐	☐	☐	☐
Frostbite Blue	☐	☐	▨	☐	☐	▨	☐	▨	▨	▨	▨	▨
Bauble Red	☐	☐	☐	☐	☐	☐	☐	☐	☐	☐	☐	☐
Limited Edition Goshi Moshi Blue		☐		☐								
Goo Green		☐		☐								
Twistmas Edition												
Brilliant Blue	☐	☐	☐	☐	☐	☐	☐	☐	☐	☐	☐	☐
Shocking Pink	☐	☐	☐	☐	☐	☐	☐	☐	☐	☐	☐	☐
Sonic Orange	☐	☐	☐	☐	☐	☐	☐	☐	☐	☐	☐	☐
Electric Yellow	☐	☐	☐	☐	☐	☐	☐	☐	☐	☐	☐	☐
Rox Collection		☐				☐						
Glitter Red Moshi Magazine Exclusive					☐			☐				
Christmas Tree Green	☐	☐	☐	☐	☐	▨	☐	☐	☐	☐	▨	☐

	1	2	3	4	5	6	7	8	9	10	11	12
Classic/Ultimate Collection/Zoo 2012												
Glitter Purple												
Glitter Orange												
Special Gold												
Glow-in-the-Dark Scream Green												
Glow-in-the-Dark Voodoo Blue												
Glow-in-the-Dark Ghost White												
Special Pumpkin Heads												
Green Two-Tone Swirl												
Red/Yellow Two-Tone Swirl												
Frostbite Blue												
Bauble Red												
Limited Edition Goshi Moshi Blue												
Goo Green												
Twistmas Edition												
Brilliant Blue												
Shocking Pink												
Sonic Orange												
Electric Yellow												
Rox Collection												
Glitter Red Moshi Magazine Exclusive												
Christmas Tree Green												

	1	2	3	4	5	6	7	8	9	10	11
Classic	✓	✓	✓	✓	✓	☐	✓	✓	✓	✓	✓
Glitter Green	☐	☐	✓	☐	☐	✓	☐	☐	✓	☐	☐
Glitter Yellow	☐	☐	☐	☐	☐	☐	☐	☐	☐	☐	☐
Special Gold	☐	☐	☐	☐	☐	☐	☐	☐	☐	☐	☐
Glow-in-the-Dark Scream Green											
Glow-in-the-Dark Voodoo Blue											
Glow-in-the-Dark Ghost White											
Special Pumpkin Heads											
Green Two-Tone Swirl				☐	☐						
Red/Yellow Two-Tone Swirl				☐	☐						
Frostbite Blue								✓	✓	✓	
Bauble Red								☐	☐	☐	
Limited Edition Goshi Moshi Blue											
Goo Green											
Twistmas Edition	✓										
Brilliant Blue	☐	☐	☐	☐	☐			☐	☐	☐	
Shocking Pink	☐	☐	☐	☐	☐		✓	☐	☐	☐	☐
Sonic Orange	☐	☐	☐			☐	☐	☐	☐	☐	
Electric Yellow	☐	☐	☐			☐	☐	☐	☐	☐	☐
Rox Collection			☐	✓	✓	✓	☐				
Christmas Tree Green								✓	☐	☐	

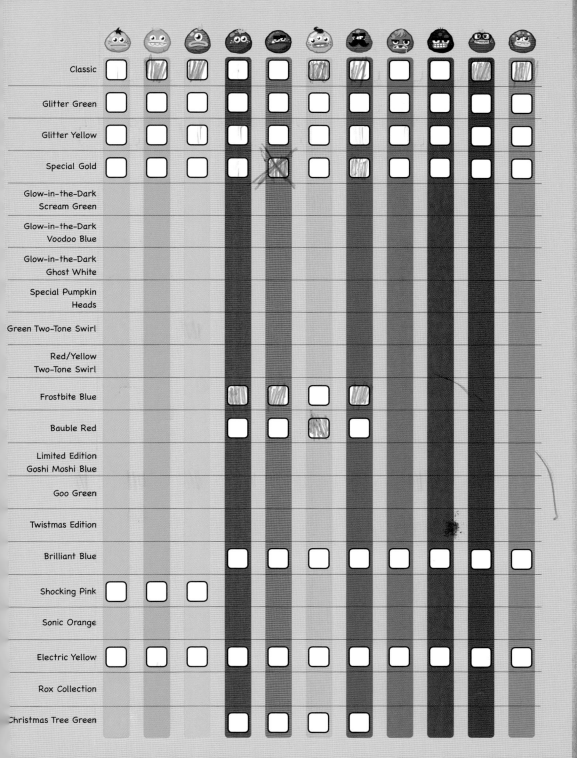

Classic	☐	▨	▨	☐	☐	▨	▨	☐	☐	▨	▨
Glitter Green	☐	☐	☐	☐	☐	☐	☐	☐	☐	☐	☐
Glitter Yellow	☐	☐	☐	☐	☐	☐	☐	☐	☐	☐	☐
Special Gold	☐	☐	☐		☒	☐	▨	☐	☐	☐	☐
Glow-in-the-Dark Scream Green											
Glow-in-the-Dark Voodoo Blue											
Glow-in-the-Dark Ghost White											
Special Pumpkin Heads											
Green Two-Tone Swirl											
Red/Yellow Two-Tone Swirl											
Frostbite Blue				▨	▨	☐	▨				
Bauble Red				☐		☐	▨	☐			
Limited Edition Goshi Moshi Blue											
Goo Green											
Twistmas Edition											
Brilliant Blue				☐	☐	☐	☐	☐	☐	☐	☐
Shocking Pink	☐	☐	☐								
Sonic Orange											
Electric Yellow	☐	☐	☐	☐	☐	☐	☐	☐	☐	☐	☐
Rox Collection											
Christmas Tree Green				☐	☐	☐	☐				

Classic	☑	☑	☑	☐	☐	☐	☐
Special Gold	☐	☐	☐	▨	☐	☐	☐
Brilliant Blue	☐			☐	☐	☐	
Shocking Pink	☐			☐	☐	☐	
Sonic Orange		☐	☐				☐
Electric Yellow		☐	☐				☐
Collectable Guide Figures Exclusive					☑		
Rox Collection					☐		

Classic	☑	☑	☑	☑	☑	☑	☑
Special Gold	☐	☐	☐	☐		☐	☐
Brilliant Blue					☐		
Shocking Pink					☐		
Sonic Orange	☐	☐	☐	☐		☐	☐
Electric Yellow	☐	☐	☐	☐		☐	☐
Collectable Guide Figures Exclusive							
Rox Collection							

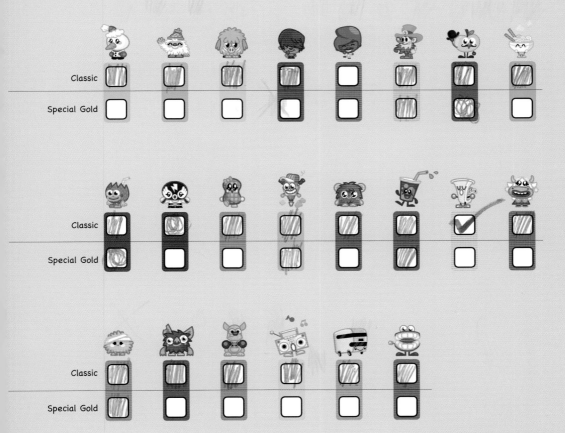

Classic

Special Gold

Classic

Special Gold

Classic

Special Gold

Stick your
photograph here

My Moshi
Collection